OFF-BEAT
SOMERSET

Dan Lees

BOSSINEY BOOKS

First published in 1986
by Bossiney Books
St Teath, Bodmin, Cornwall.
Typeset, printed and bound in Great Britain
by A. Wheaton & Co., Exeter.

Plate Acknowledgments

Front cover by Mark Bygrave
Rosemary Clinch: pages 5, 7, 8, 11, 29-32, 35-37, 41
Julia Davey: pages 9, 17, 62
Sir Arthur Guirdham: pages 20, 27
Newswest International: page 45
Gloucestershire and Avon Life: pages 48, 50, 76, 77, 82, 83, 87
Bob Bowen: page 52
T. D. Brown: pages 53, 57
Fototek, Taunton: pages 64, 65, 67, 69, backcover
Chris Harris: page 91
Michael Deering: page 93
Joe Bevan: page 59
Felicity Young: page 12
Paul Honeywill: pages 23, 71

Contents

About the Author and the Book

Dan Lees has worked as a journalist in England, Europe and America, writing about everything from crime to ballet – including a relatively insignificant war.

He settled in the Westcountry in 1970 after a spell on the French Riviera and drew on his background in Military Intelligence and journalism to write a series of spy thrillers.

At the same time he wrote features for regional publications like the *Gloucestershire and Avon Life* magazine which enabled him to indulge his curiosity about his adopted region and it was this that gave him a taste for the off-beat stories and wonderful characters of Somerset and the Westcountry, some of which he introduces in the following pages.

Arthur Guirdham, for example, the doctor who believes he has lived several times before, a grandmother who turned her hobby making dolls into a thriving business and an artist who spent a year studying a single field: all these are explored in words and pictures. The author investigates the nude paintings of Clevedon, plays the Combat Game, meets a unique family choir and takes a look at Somerset from the air together with an adventure underground.

As Dan Lees says, it is the story behind the story that he looks for. 'This is especially rewarding in the Westcountry where off-beat stories and characters are as thick on the ground today as they were centuries gone by.'

Right: **Author Dan Lees at work.**

Off-Beat Somerset

One way in which you can get a distinctly off-beat view of Somerset is to look at it through one's toes from a height of several hundred feet. At the time I was sitting in the canvas, nappy-like seat of a microlight aircraft, a motorised hang-glider put together from slim aluminium tubing and fragile fabric, with a rear mounted lawnmower engine and a wooden propellor like something out of a child's model kit.

Taking off from a field on top of Mendip was a little scary as I was quite unprepared for the machine's eagerness to leap into the sky after rolling for only a few yards across the turf on its perambulator wheels.

Once off the ground, however, the tiny aircraft flies not with the high speed and linear directness of a conventional plane, nor with the staid two dimensional progress of a balloon, or even on 'he whims of the air like a glider. No, although it may look like a Wright brothers' reject, the aircraft flies like an eagle, moving through the sky with purposeful majesty, fast enough to get you where you wish to go, slowly enough to see all there is to see, and yet so responsive to every breeze and current of air that, unencumbered by windscreen or fuselage, you become one with the plane, with the sky and with the landscape below. After a while, even the reassuring hypnotic buzz of the motor tunes itself out, turning a mundane flight into what is very nearly a mystic experience.

Seen from that height, as you look down through your outstretched legs, the landscape of Somerset looks much as it must have done for several hundred years, but you need to see it in an early morning mist to imagine how it must have looked, say, a couple of thousand years ago, with its humps, tumps, knolls, tors and downs rising from the flooded plain.

Approaching the Somerset Levels in a microlight.

For around a quarter of a million years there have been people living on the land which is slipping away beneath you and for much of the time they built themselves villages on wooden piles above the lakes or sought the lush pasturage of flood-threatened islands.

It was an unusual landscape and one which must have had an effect on the people who occupied it, making them in some ways insular because they lived on largely inaccessible islands and in other ways hospitable since a bountiful nature made it easy for them to be generous. Isolation must have helped make them singular, idiosyncratic, even eccentric, while the water, marshland and mists marked them in other ways, making it possible for them to believe – especially after a few bowls of ale or cider – that they shared their home with wraiths, sprites, ghosts and witches.

Above: **Over the hills in a microlight.** *Right:*
Off-the-beaten-track Somerset.

An off-beat land then, and one which Roman engineers were the first to try to tame, without great success, by building dykes and sea walls.

Long before the Romans came, though, to burrow Mendip for lead, the pre-historic inhabitants of the land had demonstrated their off-beat qualities by building the earliest trackways in Europe, and by raising immense fortresses, mysterious barrows and rings of stones.

Later, the Britons and the fierce warriors from the north were to enjoy the richness of the well-watered pastures and it was the Saxons who – finding that its geography made it a fine place to fatten cattle in the summer time – chose it as their 'Summer sete' so that the tribe who settled the area took the name of Summer saetas or the people of the summer place.

8

Like the Romans, the Britons and the Nordic warriors made use of the Iron Age forts, usually by building smaller encampments within their giant ramparts. One such hill fort provides a tenuous historical link with one of the most curious stories of all time – that of a Romano-British warrior chieftain who became a medieval knight many centuries after his death. To make the story even more unusual, he was then celebrated in this guise in poems, stories, paintings, plays, films and more recently television.

It seemed entirely appropriate to be flying over Arthurian territory in what the Germans call a Drachenflieger, based on a word which means dragon as well as kite, perhaps because the Roman legions flew dragon kites to frighten their enemies. The historical Arthur – if he really existed – must have lived around the sixth century and, according to legend, his main stronghold was Cadbury Castle, west of South Cadbury – an Iron Age fort dating from around 700 BC. It's an off-beat idea, or at least it was until the late 1960s when archaeologists confirmed after an extensive dig that the site had been occupied in the sixth century AD – i.e. in Arthurian times – and that post holes indicated the existence of a large feasting hall.

Could Cadbury have been Arthur's Camelot? It's an attractive idea, even if it does mean that we have to abandon our romantic notions of Arthur as a medieval knight dressed cap-à-pie in shining armour in favour of a rather less sophisticated British or Romano-British hero chieftain. And, if Cadbury is Camelot, perhaps Glastonbury is the fair Isle of Avalon since, after all, the area was once an island and at one time boats could sail from the coast right up to the town.

One persistent legend has it that Arthur will return to help his countrymen in their hour of need and this was certainly the case as far as one hard pressed bunch of twelfth-century fund raisers were concerned. Mind you, it was just a mite convenient that two skeletons which were discovered at Glastonbury were immediately identified as those of Arthur and his Queen Guinevere. In fact they couldn't have been found at a more fortunate time because when the royal remains were dug up and removed to the Great Church with much pomp and ceremony they became an instant tourist attraction – which was exactly what was needed to help raise funds for the rebuilding of the church which had been partially destroyed by the great fire of 1184.

Anachronistically, the men of the twelfth century dressed Arthur, his knightly companions and their consorts in the armour, robes and gowns of their own time and it is in this guise that Arthur returned yet again to imbue generations of English boys and girls with notions of honour and chivalry. Recently he has returned once more, this time perhaps more accurately portrayed for television as a Romano-British warrior chieftain battling against the Saxons.

Perhaps the real Arthur had a lot in common with Harold Godwinson – the cider drinking Anglo-Saxon who was defeated by William the Conqueror in 1066 and whose sons, in true Somerset fashion, were still trying to regain their father's kingdom at Montacute in 1068, long after most of the fighting was finished. Even so, the chivalrous King Arthur and his Knights of the Round Table remain imperishable figures and it isn't difficult to imagine

Montacute.

Wellington Monument.

the Arthurian legends growing up around Glastonbury, a place of mists and strange forces where disbelief is easily suspended.

In fact, if the microlight I was flying had turned into a time machine and glided over medieval Glastonbury the sight would have scarcely been thought worthy of comment – apart perhaps from a disparaging remark about the silly beggars from Malmesbury way being up to their daft tricks again. After all, if you have had Joseph of Arimathea, and perhaps Jesus Christ as well, as visitors you are not going to be much impressed by a mere U.F.O.

Joseph is said to have sailed up to Glastonbury in the course of a trading mission and to have brought the young Jesus with him as an apprentice. When he stuck his staff into the ground it mysteriously took root and blossomed and has done so every year at Christmas time to commemorate the visit.

The mists, and the mysterious forces generated by thousands of years of religious observances going back way beyond Joseph's supposed visit, may account for the legends of Glastonbury but elsewhere the mists have usually had help from the Westcountry's regional beverage – cider.

Almost every mention of ancient customs, markets, meetings and get-togethers of any sort includes a reference to the large quantities of strong ale or cider – usually the latter – which were consumed on those occasions, and there were plenty of feast days, holy days, saints' days and the rest from which to choose. In Somerset cider was an everyday drink as well as an accompaniment to special festivities, so it could have been responsible for many of the wonders, prodigies, monsters, wraiths and spirits that go to make up the off-beat history of the region. After all, there's no telling what people may or may not have seen on their way home from ceremonies like that of the Ashen Faggot, when the bursting of each band tying the burning bundle of ash logs was celebrated with huge draughts of cider or 'egg hot', a mixture of eggs, cider and spices.

Cheese, which formed a major part of the Somerset diet, could also have been responsible for the odd dream or two, some of which may have been realistic enough to have been related as fact.

Left: **The Wellington Monument drawn by Felicity Young.**

Certainly there were one or two unusual customs connected with the substance which came to be known as 'milk made immortal', one being that girls were given the first slice of a cheese to ensure that they would bear children.

As for cider, its making began on All Saints Day, 1 November, and it was considered unlucky to make it on St Dunstan's Day, 19 May, and presumably at any time after that date. Then there were wassailing ceremonies to ensure a good crop, usually entailing extensive sampling of the previous year's product, together with the firing of guns to scare off evil spirits – and you can't get much more off-beat than that.

Come to think of it, cider could be at the bottom of many Somerset mysteries, including perhaps one or two of the prehistoric mounds which seem to serve no useful purpose. Of course they could be tokens of esteem for the Great Earth Mother or signals to catch the attention of visiting aliens but on the other hand they could just as easily have been the cider inspired monument of some Iron Age ruler who, after a night of carousal, thought that building a record size mound was a 'good idea' and was too proud to abandon his plan in the cool light of morning.

Later 'follies' – and there are plenty of them around – could also have been inspired by cider but were more likely the result of a few too many glasses of claret or port. Four of them, however, situated at Barwick Park, have a much more laudable raison d'etre since they were erected by a Mr George Messiter in the early nineteenth century with the aim of providing work for unemployed glove makers.

That particular solution to the unemployment problem may sound a little strange to us nowadays but a couple of hundred years ago there must have been plenty of work to be had building follies, sham castles and monuments and no doubt quite a few of them were erected in order to make work. One monument which may have been designed partly to help out men on hard times after the Napoleonic Wars is the Wellington Obelisk on the Blackdown Hills which has to be one of the most off-beat monuments in history since it commemorates a virtually non-existent connection between Arthur Wellesley and the town whose name he chose when he was ennobled.

The victorious general picked the name partly because it had the same initial letter as his family name and partly because of a tenuous family connection with the village of Wellesley near Wells. There was no other association but the people of Wellington were nevertheless proud of his choice and he was given some property in the area in an attempt to justify it, although he only visited it once.

Amid the heady euphoria following Waterloo it was decided to erect a monument to Wellington on the Blackdown Hills and an architect called Thomas Lee from Barnstaple was commissioned to design it. Two years after the decisive battle the foundation stone was laid with great pomp and ceremony, watched by a crowd of ten thousand people who later marched down the hill, with the Clayhidon Band at their head, to celebrate the event in the approved fashion with plenty of cider and strong ale.

Unfortunately, Wellington's popularity didn't last and, in spite of continuous appeals, subscriptions for the building of the monument were not forthcoming at anything like the rate the organisers had hoped. Because of this, Thomas Lee was asked to trim the cost and came up with the idea of reducing the proposed four-sided monument to a three-sided affair which, although it gave the resulting column, quite fortuitously, the appearance of a British bayonet of the time, failed to effect the necessary economies. In the end, after ten years, the project was abandoned and the unfinished monument was left to the mercy of wind, rain and thunderstorms; indeed at one stage the structure was so badly damaged by lightning it looked as though it could never be resurrected.

However, as the clerics of Glastonbury had discovered centuries before when a long dead Arthur and Guinevere provided a happy boost for their funds, the Wellington Monument Committee were to find it easier to raise money to perpetuate the memory of a dead hero than to celebrate the triumphs of a live one. When Wellington died his political sins were largely forgiven. Instead, the citizens of Wellington remembered the Duke's generous subscriptions to various local projects like schools and hospitals, and new fund-raising appeals for the monument were launched with considerable success. Work on the monument was restarted and it was built up to a height of 170 feet – to which later restoration was to add another few feet – and given a pointed top which heightened the resemblance to a bayonet.

That should have been the end of the matter but, if the Wellington Monument itself formed the basis of an odd little story,

15

it was the Waterloo guns which made the affair genuinely off-beat. The story of the guns began when it was decided to surround the monument with twenty four brass cannon which had been captured at Waterloo by Wellington's armies and which, it was felt, would add an appropriate and decorative touch. The twenty four cannon were to be sent from Woolwich arsenal and in 1818 fifteen guns were in fact unloaded at Exeter.

However, there were a couple of minor discrepancies – apart from the number of guns having been reduced by nine – in so far as the cannon themselves had apparently suffered a mysterious sea change. For one thing, the guns which arrived at Exeter were iron guns instead of the brass cannon that had been agreed upon, and for another, they had never been anywhere near Waterloo. Even more curiously, the iron guns were part of a shipment of weapons ordered by Catherine the Great from a Scottish foundry before the end of the eighteenth century.

Perhaps there was an ex-artillery man on the Monument Committee or maybe it was simply that the members recognised the difference between iron and brass. Whatever the reason, they refused to pay for the onward transport of the incorrect guns, even when Exeter Corporation threatened to sell them. In fact the guns remained in Exeter for nearly a hundred years until in 1910 four of them were moved to the Wellington monument where they remained until the Second World War when they were commandeered for scrap to help the war effort. They were never used for this purpose and, for some reason or other, were instead given an honourable burial – at Watchet.

One of these days when I get around to writing the story of off-beat Devon I shall try to find out what became of the remaining eleven of Catherine the Great's iron guns, why they either didn't reach her or were sent back to England in the first place – and perhaps also what happened to the original twenty four brass cannon.

Of course it's the cannon which make the story of Wellington's monument a typically off-beat Somerset, or for that matter Westcountry, story by providing that extra dimension of the almost

Right: **'I have had the opportunity to take a leisurely look ...'**

incredible which makes the yarn that much more interesting.

In my experience this extra dimension, whether it be the co-incidental, the unbelievable, the mysterious or simply the serendipitous, is a characteristic of Somerset stories and a characteristic which makes working as a writer and journalist in the county so rewarding.

There's always a little something to add; some little off-beat detail, even if the story is 6,000 years old. For instance, the fact that the Eclipse Track at Shapwick is amongst the oldest trackways in the world, and as such a precursor of the railways, is a good yarn, but finding the oldest English longbow at the side of the track makes it even better. In the same way, the finding of Iron Age bone dice and a shaker on the site adds a touch of human interest to the story of the Glastonbury Lake Village.

As a journalist, the most pleasant aspect of working as a feature writer for newspapers and magazines is that you have more time to explore these curious details and to look for the story behind the story than when you are a reporter working on what is known as 'hard' news. This is especially gratifying and rewarding in the Westcountry where off-beat stories and characters are as thick on the ground today as they were in centuries gone by.

My great good fortune has been that as a writer for many different publications I have had the opportunity to take a leisurely look at some of the more unusual people and places in the region. At one time, for instance, I was working very nearly full time as a ghost hunter for an American publication – a task which took me into several ancient Somerset buildings. On one occasion I even provided the off-beat element myself when my amateur photograph of the interior of a 'haunted' church revealed what appeared to be a ghostly figure standing in the pulpit. I didn't claim that it was anything other than incompetent photography but the Americans loved it and besides, in Somerset – who knows?

The Somerset Heretics

My friend Arthur Guirdham firmly believes that he has lived several times before his present existence and that he has walked the earth as a Roman slave girl, a thirteenth century Cathar heretic and as a French sailor who was captured and imprisoned by the English at the time of the Napoleonic Wars.

His is an off-beat story, to say the least, especially in view of the fact that he is able to back up his assertions with masses of remarkable evidence, much of which seems difficult, if not impossible, to challenge. It becomes even more unusual in the case of his Cathar re-incarnation because over the years he has found himself at the centre of a multiple re-incarnation of people now living in Somerset, all of whom seem to have had a previous existence in southern France some seven centuries ago.

Quite independently, all eight members of the group had tuned in to a series of tragic events which took place in the Languedoc region of France in the years 1242-1244. Arthur Guirdham, who appears to have acted as a sort of catalyst through which the members of the group shared their experience of a previous existence, was able to discover the medieval names of seven out of the eight people involved, together with the roles they played in the story.

It's a story that is certainly off-beat enough, but what makes it completely fascinating is the fact that Arthur Guirdham – far from being the sort of credulous person who sees ghosts every time a stair creaks and is determined to see the hand of the supernatural in every trivial coincidence – is a much respected psychiatrist who until his retirement was Senior Psychiatric Consultant to a group of Somerset hospitals. Not only that but, as I learned when I met him, he is a cultured, well-read, well-travelled man and a professional sceptic who is inclined to discount even what appears to be good evidence for his case if he feels that it cannot be substantiated.

Of course when I met him for the first time at his home in the small village of Bathford I had no idea that he was as respected in his own field as turned out to be the case. However, even before I had finished my first glass of sherry, I was aware that he was a man to be taken seriously and one who, no matter how keen to vindicate his ideas, would be meticulous in his search for the truth.

The story he had to tell was a strange one and had begun in 1962 when he was consulted professionally by a woman he named Mrs Smith. She had been referred to him by her own doctor because she was suffering from recurrent nightmares which were accompanied by piercing cries, so strident that her husband was forced to wake her for fear she would rouse the whole neighbourhood. It appeared that she had been having the same frightening dream for more than twenty years – she was then in her thirties – and each time had dreamed that she was lying on the floor of her room when a man came in from her right whose approach filled her with terror.

The nightmare, said Dr Guirdham, was not a particularly interesting one but it did remind him of a terrible dream he had had himself for several years in which a tall man approached the place where he was sleeping and leaned over him causing him to become petrified with fear.

At that time no mention had been made either by Mrs Smith or by Dr Guirdham of the Cathars or anything concerning the sect although the doctor himself had felt drawn to the countryside of the Languedoc in Southern France and was becoming increasingly interested in the Cathars and their fate. At the same time he was involved in tracing his ancestry and in finding out more about an Augustinian order called the Bonhommes who settled in Bristol during the thirteenth century – the name Bonhommes or Good Men being the affectionate name given to Cathar priests of the Languedoc by the people for whom they officiated. He was also interested in the theory that the English Royal House, especially the Black Prince (1330-1376) had supported if not joined the Cathars and may therefore have allowed them to establish themselves in this country.

The Cathars were a sect who practised a primitive form of

Left: **'Arthur Guirdham firmly believes that he has lived several times before.'**

21

Christianity which at least as far as the laity was concerned was simple and uncomplicated without any of the sophisticated ritual of the Catholic Church. They were Duallists who believed that the world was created by the Devil and that life was a perpetual struggle between Good and Evil. In this way they explained the paradox of an omniscient, omnipotent Deity who permitted misery and suffering – a paradox which the orthodox Christians believed was explained by God's wishing to strengthen human beings by testing them in the flame of suffering.

Cathar priests and priestesses called Parfaits and Parfaites – the perfect ones – by their adherents often practised healing and were skilled in the use of medicinal herbs and plants. They were much closer to their flock than the members of the Catholic hierarchy and their simplicity of behaviour and dress was in great contrast to the greed, hypocrisy and rampant immorality of many of the Catholic clergy of the time.

As an heretical sect, however, they were the natural targets of the Inquisition and many of them were tortured and died of their ill treatment or were executed on the orders of the inquisitors who themselves were not permitted to shed blood. For the Cathars, the soul could be liberated from the domination of the flesh and once so liberated could exist independent of time and space. In other words, they believed in re-incarnation and it was largely because of this belief that they were massacred without mercy.

It was not until 1965 that Mrs Smith told Doctor Guirdham that she had recognised him from the time of her first consultation as a man she had first met in the thirteenth century. Even so, it was some time before she told him all the circumstances but she did tell him that he had taken refuge from a violent snow storm in her father's house near Toulouse. Apparently her family was in very modest circumstances and before the night of the storm she had never seen anyone like him as he belonged to a family of minor aristocrats.

Said Dr Guirdham, 'It seems that I spent the night there, sleeping on the floor of the one roomed cottage. The girl, who was still an

Right: **'Each time she dreamed that she was lying on the floor when a man came in from her right whose approach filled her with terror.'**

adolescent, stayed awake to watch over me and after a while slid furtively towards me and kissed my hand. It seems that she had fallen in love with me at first sight – which I must say is something that has never happened to me in my present incarnation.'

Doctor Guirdham continued to meet people who mentioned or were interested in the Cathars, many more, he insists, than could be ascribed to mere coincidence. He met, for example, a senior RAF officer who told him that while walking on the lower slopes of the mount of Montsegur with his wife they had both been gripped by 'an inexplicable terror'. At the time the officer had never heard of the Cathars and was quite unaware of the fact that he had walked on the spot where two hundred members of the sect were burned at the stake in 1244.

'It seemed,' said Dr Guirdham, 'that I was acting as some sort of magnet for anyone concerned with the Cathars.'

By this time Mrs Smith was no longer suffering from the nightmares which had been the start of the whole affair but she had begun to dream in French. She had also visited France and had been terrified by the atmosphere she felt in Toulouse – the city which was the 'Rome of the Cathar heresy' and as such a special target of the Inquisition.

She began to write down her dream experiences and observations of the thirteenth century, often expressing her surprise at details which would have been well-known to scholars of the period – like the fact that no wine glasses were in use at that time and that the hearths of the houses were in the middle of the floor.

She wrote that she had left her family to live with Roger, although they had not married, and added that he had told her repeatedly that if anything happened to him she should go 'to Fabrissa'. She didn't know whether Fabrissa was a person or a place.

She also revealed that during a dream – as her husband told her later – she had begun to scream while shouting about the crypt of the Cathedral of St Etienne in Toulouse, which she pronounced Tolosa – the name of Toulouse in langue d'oc. It was in this crypt that many Cathars were interrogated and tortured by the Inquisition. Mrs Smith had made a definite identification of Dr Guirdham as Roger and after a while more named individuals began to occur in her dreams of thirteenth-century France.

It was then that Dr Guirdham began to take the dreams and their implication of re-incarnation seriously since, by using the extensive records of the Inquisition available in academic libraries in the Toulouse area – to which Mrs Smith had no access – he was able to identify several of the people she mentioned as historical personages.

Mrs Smith was even coming up with the correct spellings of names current in the Languedoc region in the thirteenth century, like Alais and Fabrissa who was in fact a person and the aunt of the man in the first recurring nightmare.

Mrs Smith was also recording accurate details of thirteenth-century life which would normally have been known only to serious scholars of the period and, what was more, details of Cathar rites and observances which were not then known even to the experts but which were subsequently proved to be correct. For instance, she described in detail the robes of Cathar priests, insisting, for example, that Roger's clothing was dark blue in colour, whereas all the experts had asserted that Cathar priests invariably wore black. It was not until much later that a French student of Catharism proved conclusively that the priests also wore blue.

For some time Dr Guirdham found it difficult to credit some of Mrs Smith's revelations, such as her assurance that as Roger he had been given pieces of sugar when he was ill. It was only later that he discovered that loaf sugar – so valuable it was kept as she had described under lock and key – had been recommended by thirteenth-century doctors for pulmonary complaints. It was shortly after the death of Roger from a lung condition, aggravated by torture, that Mrs Smith herself joined the other martyrs of Montsegur, an event of which she was able, seven centuries later, to give a convincing account.

In order to determine the historical authenticity of Mrs Smith's account, Dr Guirdham felt he had to make a complete identification of the personages in her dreams, the area in which they lived and the period. This he was able to do by using reference books like *The History of The Inquisition in The Middle Ages* by Guiraud and a collection of records in the Bibliotheque Nationale in Paris. With these documents he was able to prove the existence of the principal personages in the dreams i.e. Roger (himself), Alais, Fabrissa and Pierre de Mazarolles. He was also helped extensively by French historians including those who had made a specialised study of the Cathar heresy.

In the early 1970s Doctor Guirdham came into contact with the

Cathars once more when an acquaintance of his wife asked him casually if the names Raymond and Albigensian had any special significance, to which he was able to reply that Raymond was the name of the Comtes of Toulouse and Albigensian was the name of the Cathar heresy which flourished in their territories during the thirteenth century.

Later the woman, who he called Miss Mills, was subjected to a bombardment of voices, first in dreams and later in a half-sleeping, half-waking state. The voices insisted that she should confide in Dr Guirdham who says that by this time, 'I felt that dramatic and almost physical methods were being used to draw my attention to Catharism and the thirteenth century.'

In 1971, says Dr Guirdham, 'things became exciting' as Miss Mills began writing down – while asleep – the messages and experiences of her dreams. Once again, as in the case of Mrs Smith, Miss Mills dreamed and recorded details which could have been known only to experts, together with many facts which were not known even to students of the period but which were later proved to have been correct. She was also able to give details of the siege of the fortress of Montsegur, including the names of the men at arms who elected to die with the Cathars after the surrender of the castle and even to explore such byways as the nature of the wounds caused by medieval projectiles and the treatments used to heal them.

As in the case of Mrs Smith, Dr Guirdham was able to confirm and verify information derived by Miss Mills 'from the spirit world' which was proved to coincide exactly with that derived from records and other worldly sources. While doing so he was brought into contact with several other people living in twentieth-century Somerset who, like Mrs Smith and Miss Mills, appeared to have lived and suffered as Cathars in medieval France. He published his findings in a book called *We Are One Another,* published by Neville Spearman, which is when an American newspaper commissioned me to interview him and write the story.

As I have already mentioned, I was extremely impressed by Dr Guirdham's academic qualifications and experience, together with his evident sincerity. Not only that, but the welter of detail – of which I have had the space to record only a tiny fraction – wore away at my natural scepticism. There was, I felt, no question whatsoever of fraud and if the whole thing had been a question of multiple illusion and self-deception then it had been incredibly

**Montsegur – a
Somerset link?**

detailed and sustained as well as involving the participation of
several people rather than just one individual.

Even so I do take a lot of convincing on such matters and with Dr
Guirdham's consent – though without giving details of my
intentions – I contacted several leading authorities on the Cathars
and the thirteenth century, including the then Professor of History
at the University of Toulouse. For academics, and especially
French academics, their replies were positive and straightforward.
'Yes,' they told me, 'the details recorded by the "Somerset Cathars"
had been surprisingly accurate and in some cases had ante-dated
their own discoveries and researches.'

As for this particular Doubting Thomas, I shall still be asking for
further proof when being enrolled for my first harp lesson or being
roasted to a crisp at Regulo 8, but I have to admit that, as off-beat
stories go, it's a cracker.

A Nude Look at Clevedon

Help!

There's a naked lady floating in a ballon over Clevedon Bowling Green – but don't worry; she's quite decorous, and more than a little charming. In fact, in the days when railway posters were more of an art form than they are today, she would probably have ended up proclaiming the resort's delights to the inhabitants of the shivering north.

The young woman appears in the same state of undress conducting a surprisingly blasé orchestra on the Green Beach band stand – and in several other well-known corners throughout the town, like the churchyard and the park.

In these days of Page Three Girls and full-frontal TV, the young lady is about as daring as bare legs on a piano but curiously, her innocent pink and white form still comes as something of a shock when juxtaposed with Clevedon's Victorian villas. This, of course, is precisely what her creator was aiming for, and the inspiration for her full series of sixteen paintings of the town, which she began when she arrived in Clevedon at the age of thirty some six years ago.

Ann Jenkins, who signs her paintings simply 'A. J.', explains her motives: 'When I first came here I thought that to paint a nude in this sort of environment would present a real contrast. Of course people are prepared to accept nudes in a landscape in old paintings, but in a contemporary landscape it still gives them something of a shock.'

Ann exhibited some of her paintings recently at the Clevedon Pier Preservation Trust's pier tollhouse, and found people were not so

Right: **Ann Jenkins.**

**'... music-lovers who study the bandstand
orchestra will be surprised to find Pablo
Casals on cello.'**

much shocked as intrigued to find that while they could not identify
the imaginary nude, they knew many of the other figures. Ann has
depicted several of her friends, together with some well-known
Clevedon characters, and music-lovers who study the bandstand
orchestra will be surprised to find Pablo Casals on cello.

Even some of the town's better-known dogs are featured, like the
poodle from the Fallen Tree pub who is shown sneaking off with a
stolen leg of lamb. The pictures are so detailed that each one takes
some five to six weeks to complete.

Ann rejects frames, which she regards as restrictive and inclined
to turn paintings into furnishings. And as she is determined that the
subject should dictate the shape of her works, her paintings turn out
to be triangular, multi-sided or round, as the fancy takes her.

'Even some of the town's better known dogs
are featured ...'

'There's a naked lady floating in a balloon over Clevedon Bowling Green ...'

Ann might never have become an artist had not her original career as a ballet dancer come to a sudden end when she badly damaged her knee while dancing the twist. At the time she was seventeen and training at the Ballet Rambert Dance School. 'In those days,' said Ann, 'we had formal schooling in the mornings only and every afternoon was spent on dancing – which probably explains why I had no 'A' levels.

'I went to Cheltenham Art College where I got a low grade in Art but married an artist and had three children – two boys and a girl. I moved to Clevedon when the marriage broke up and that's when I started to paint. I painted a small picture called "Caught Out" as a gift for a friend and included the naked lady among the players in a village cricket match, but it was not until later that I realised how much I had been influenced by my reading of Jungian psychology and that the woman was his universal female figure – the "Anima".

'It's a concept which has been used in many paintings but usually in a negative way as, say, a witch. My naked lady is much more positive; she's not a Page Three Girl and there is nothing meek, weak or purely derivative about her. She is firmly in the centre of things, whether she's in a balloon or conducting an orchestra. When the paintings were shown for the first time at the Toll House in Clevedon, people had a real giggle, which is what I like; paintings shouldn't be elitist; they should be colourful – a celebration of life.'

Ann's paintings are certainly colourful and were much acclaimed at subsequent exhibitions but her production remains low, mainly because she so much enjoys her other off-beat occupation – as a designer and maker of furniture.

The Clevedon series, prints of which, mounted on wood, will soon be on sale in local bookshops and art stores, has a great deal of naive, refreshing charm. But there is nothing naive about Ann who, with the exception of two of the paintings which were sold to 'buy wood', is hanging on to the originals.

After all, if the idea catches on, *Déjeuner sur L'Esplanade de Clevedon* could one day be worth real money.

OBS–C

The Queen's Camel and the Wild Boars of Evercreech

I'd love to live in Nempnett Thrubwell, Westonzoyland or any of the many Somerset places with names that roll off the tongue like poetry, full of mystery, sonority and the occasional flash of humour.

How pleasing it would be, for instance, to be able to reply to banal questions about one's address with a regal 'Queen's Camel', an erudite 'Stowey juxta Clutton' or a confusing 'Congresbury'.

The fact is that in a country full of off-beat place names those of Somerset are among the most unusual, possibly because each succeeding wave of early settlers stayed long enough to make its contribution to the nomenclature and because they included Celts as well as Nordic and Norman invaders. This meant that there was often linguistic confusion as well as the delightful Chinese Whispers syndrome to ensure that place names of the area were as interesting and amusing as they could possibly be.

I suppose everyone knows the party game of Chinese Whispers in which a phrase is transmitted in whispers from one guest to another, often suffering an amusing sea change in the process. The most famous example is supposed to have originated not at some bibulous party but in the Western Desert where, at a time when radio silence was being observed by our troops, a verbal message was sent back from a forward position by whispers from one man to the next. Unfortunately the message which started out as 'Send reinforcements; we are going to advance' became garbled in transmission so that the officer commanding the reserves was surprised to receive the request, 'Send three and fourpence; we are going to a dance.'

Right: '... names that roll off the tongue ...'

34

'Another little beauty of a name is Congres-bury ...'

In ancient times, when writing was either unheard of or was the jealously guarded craft of a handful of clerks and scribes, the only way in which information like place names could be transmitted was verbally and, even when writing became more general, spelling was, to say the least, arbitrary, which meant that it added to rather than reduced the possibilities of error and confusion.

Again at the time when most of our hamlets were named it was not merely different languages that made things difficult. There was no such thing as standard English – or standard Celtic for that matter – so that each parish might have had a slightly different dialect from that of its neighbour. In these conditions it was easy for names to become confused, especially as there were other influences at work, like our compulsion to shorten and simplify names wherever possible and to insist that names which sound as though they ought to mean something really do mean what they sound like.

Fortunately for the amateur place name enthusiast, the incredible number of influences which have gone to make up most of our place names means that in many instances his guess can be as good as or even better than the work of the most erudite scholar as nobody can really say for sure how the particular name came about.

There have even been cases where the instincts of ordinary folk and their long-standing traditions have proved correct while the version of a name insisted upon by the better educated was selected merely because it appeared to make academic sense. As James Hill put it in his *Place Names Of Somerset*, 'Many local pronunciations, esteemed vulgar, are in fact correct. Stowey for example is called Stawy, which goes back to the ancient name of Stal-wei.' It was changed to Stowey by the literate who knew there were many 'Stow' names and thought the locals must have got it wrong. 'Stow' itself means a place and one book the interested amateur will find useful is the *Oxford Dictionary of Place Names* which not only lists most

'I'd love to live in Westonzoyland ...'

English ones, together with their derivations, but includes items on each of the much used name elements like 'Stow'. These crop up time and time again – often eroded by mispronunciation, misspelling or misunderstanding but still enabling us to hazard a guess at the meaning of a place name.

Although the guess is often as good as the opinion of the most erudite student of nomenclature it is as well to consult the experts if you wish to go deeply into the question. After all, you can always make up your own mind when you have all the facts and no philologist can do much better. It's easy however to be a little over-confident. 'Cam' for example is an element cropping up in many river names, meaning bent or crooked – in fact it's tempting to see a connection with cam shaft – and explains, for example, the delightful Queen's Camel and Abbot's Camel as well as the less exotic sounding Cameley.

How easy and obvious to see the same element in Camerton – the town on the bend of the river – what could be more logical. Unfortunately this particular 'Cam' is part of a personal name – Gamalhere – a fact which is easier to appreciate when one learns that Camerton sometimes appears in old documents as Camelarton.

River names of course frequently occur as parts of place names, often with the original meaning of water – like 'afon' from which we got Avon. Sometimes when a place changed hands the incoming victors would adopt the full name of the river, thinking it to be simply a pleasant name, adding their own word for river, which led to tautologies meaning the river River or even the river River River. Sometimes the river was given the name of a god, like the 'Chew' in Chewton Mendip, Chewton Magna, Chew Stoke and so on, which appears in the Domesday Book as 'Chiu' and is thought to be associated with the same Norse god who gave us Tuesday – the day of Tiw.

Somerset is and was a watery area and the place names reflect it with elements like 'ean' – a Celtic root associated with water and with the Welsh 'afon' – appearing in names such as Winsham, Wincalleton and Wincanton, with Wincalleton being particularly watery since 'cale' is also a river name.

Then there are the Somerset rhines that troubled poor Monmouth at the Battle of Sedgemoor and which have their analogue in the German Rhine or Rhein, not to mention the Rhone, the Rhin and the Rijn. There's also a strong suggestion that all of them are linked with rain via the old Gothic 'rign' and the Old Frisian 'rein' – which could mean that Cockneys have the right of it. Wrington is another 'rhine' or 'rhin' word so Wrington is the town on the rhine.

More fun still is the water word that appears in Axbridge or the bridge over the water and is related to 'Usk', 'uisge' and 'Wisge' – which recall the water of life or 'uisge beatha' in the Gaelic. There's also a distant connection with 'aqua' as in Aqua Sulis which means that Axbridge is related to Bath.

Talking of bridges, one of them at least is something of a snare and that's the bridge in Bridgwater which turns out to have nothing to do with bridges and precious little to do with water. It seems the 'bridg' bit is really the same word as 'burgh' while the water part comes from the personal name of Walter de Donai – which makes it Walter's town and just goes to show that you can't even rely on bad spelling when it comes to the 'obvious'.

With all the water in Somerset, especially before drainage and sea walls had their effect, it's not surprising that there were a lot of islands around, although some of them now wear curious and misleading disguises. Nailsea, for instance, which appears to the unwary amateur to contain something like the German for lake, turns out to be exactly the opposite as the name was originally Nigelsig or Nigelsey – which makes it Nigel's Island, although Nigel does sound a little up market for Saxon Somerset.

The Saxon 'ig' and 'ey' crop up all over the place in Somerset and they are a gift to amateur place name enthusiasts. For example, I was extremely pleased once I had come across the 'ey' ending to have my guess about Muchelney confirmed. It really is the 'muckle ey' or big island as in 'many a mickle makes a muckle' and somewhere there ought to be a Mickleney. There's certainly an Athelney, which again I guessed right as Prince's Island or the Island of the Aethling.

In fact I was feeling pretty pleased with myself by the time I tackled Glastonbury, one of the most famous names in the whole county and came up with glass town burgh. Apparently this is one even the experts argue about which means that your guess is as good as mine and very nearly as good as theirs. There's one school of thought which holds that Glastonbury began life as something like Glastonia, meaning the place where the woad grows, from the

Celtic word 'glastus' for woad, to which was added the Old English 'ieg' – which is yet another island – and burgh giving us 'the place of the people where the woad grows'.

But what of the Welsh Ineswytrin which is also found as a name for the place and is a direct translation of 'the island of glass' with 'ines', 'insel', 'insular' related to the first element and 'wytrin' related to vitrium, vitrine and vitrious? Glas-ton-bury... the town on the island of glass – what could be more simple except that it doesn't seem to mean anything. The glass does become a little clearer – sorry – when one learns that 'wytrin' means glass not only in the modern sense but also in its primary meaning of green, blue or grey in colour, making Glastonbury the town on the greeny-grey-blue island – which is poetic if nothing else.

Unfortunately nothing is simple in off-beat Somerset nomenclature and, as it happens, the Latin 'vitrum' also means woad. Mind you, woad – also known as the dyer's weed – did have a rather pretty blue colour... so, back to place of the people of the island where the woad grows!

Another little beauty of a name is Congresbury which some people associate with St Conger who is said to have been buried there. All that is known about St Conger or Congar is that there was a hermit of that name who came from the east – Saint by the way being a tricky little title which implied holiness rather than actual canonisation, as in 'the man's a saint'. Anyway, alas for St Conger, the popular pronunciation of 'Congsbury' could be nearer the mark, although no one can be certain whether this gives the inhabitants the cachet of living in the place of the King's garth – from the Saxon 'cyng-gar' – or the less regal distinction of having homes in the place of the rabbit warren – from the Celtic 'y cwining gaer', the main word of which is related to coney.

A more likely saint is St Kew of Kew Stoke – as opposed to Chew Stoke – who lived in the hollow of a hill above the village near Weston-super-Mare, close to which is the path of St Kew.

There was also a St Keyn, but Keyn is a personal name so there need not have been any holy man involved. It's one for the experts to argue about, like Wellington, which some people derive from Weland – the Saxon Vulcan – while the *Oxford Dictionary of English Place Names* derives it from the Old English 'Weo-lah' meaning a temple.

Personal names account for a lot of place names, many of which

**' "Cam" for example is an element cropping
up in many river names ...'**

seem at first sight to have a more interesting origin. There's
Cadbury Camp, for example, which could be 'Cad' from 'Cadaer',
meaning fort, but is thought more likely to have been Cadda's
Place, as in Catsash and Catcott.

Creeks and Combes are favourite components too and though, as
James Hill puts it 'the wild boar no longer frequents Evercreech'
it's pleasing to spot the association with the Anglo-Saxon 'eofer' and
the German 'Eber'. Combe, as in Gatcombe and Brockley Combe is
a pleasing sound and it's fun to imagine Brock the badger playing
on the lea, although once again one has to remember that people
often took the names of animals so Brock could have been a
person.

Harptree provides another splendid series of names and conjures
up visions of an ancient harpist playing under a lone tree although
'tre' is, in fact, a Celtic homestead and the harp is more likely to

have come from the 'haerepath' or war path – the way of the army.

Imagination has often made names more amusing than they really are – as in the case of Beggar's Bush and Beggar Quarm which derive from the personal name Bega, and the name Rodway, as in Rodway Fitspaine, which has nothing to do with roadway and everything to do with a gentleman called Brodwig whose name crops up again in Bruadstoke or Radstock, while – alas for legend – Hornblotton is simply Heribald's place.

Worse still, Waterlip in East Cranmore which sounds as if it ought to refer to a superb waterfall is merely the 'laib', or inheritance, of the ubiquitous Walter – remember Bridgwater.

So what about dear old Nempnett Thrubwell, one of the most off-beat names of all? Surely that can't have a mundane explanation? Thrubwell, it seems, is a form of thorpe which is related to the German 'Dorf' and means a small village. Nempnett, the popular pronunciation of which is or used to be Niblett, is more elusive. It could be Nehemia's or Nym's hut, or it could come from Empnete since Emp was a personal name, in which case it would be Empans et or Emp's headland.

Compared with some of the places we've looked at it seems to be something of a banal explanation for such a promising and unusual name; unless of course you care to go in search of the presumably Christian 'Nehemia' or the almost certainly pagan 'Emp', which could take you into a whole new region of off-beat Somerset.

Upstairs Downstairs

It was not exactly a 'Voyage to the Centre of the Earth'. But a mile from the surface, sitting on a rock in a stalactite-decked cavern the height of a medium-sized cathedral, it certainly felt like it.

The whole thing began, innocently enough, with a suggestion that we should undertake a middle-of-the-road Mendip caving excursion, between the leisurely conducted walks of the tourist caves and the rough descents of the skilled and fully-equipped caver. If there were such a cave, I told expert Tony Atkinson, it would let me examine the possibilities of caving as a family sport – and, quite coincidentally, complete some last-minute research for my new crime novel.

In retrospect, I can only assume that it was the drinks at Tony's Mendip pub that made the prospect of such an expedition seem a good idea, and I had forgotten the whole thing when he phoned to say that he had laid everything on for the following Sunday. 'Just wear some old clothes and bring a stout pair of boots,' he said. The stoutest pair of boots in my wardrobe turned out to be a pair of fleece-lined fashion jobs designed to supplement the car heater, but they looked sturdy enough, and, after all, we were only going to have a quiet look at the sport, not break records.

On Sunday, together with the photographer Tony Ferrand – there was to be a slightly confusing trio of Tonys – I met up with Tony Atkinson and Tony Mintram, and set off for a cave some four or five miles from Green Ore, on the edge of Tyning's Farm high in the hills. There we kitted up in coveralls and helmets, with lamps powered by battery packs and knotted belts which slid easily round the body.

Springing lightly over a five-barred gate, I made my way with the others to a largish hollow, in the middle of which stood a steel-doored concrete bunker – as innocent an entrance to another world as Dr Who's police box. Inside there was a short drop down to a steel ladder leading into a sharply descending narrow passageway which presented few problems, apart from being floored with rocks covered in exceedingly slippery mud. Even so, after a few minutes of rather ungainly progress, including a section which involved sliding over unforgiving rocks on one's bottom, and another which, in my innocence, I thought painfully narrow, I was glad to reach a largish chamber where there was room to breathe and stand upright. There were even a couple of strategically-placed rocks on which to sit and recover strength for the return trip.

As Tony Atkinson pointed out the remains of a stalactite 'curtain,' and explained how the tips, which take a thousand years to grow an inch, had been vandalised by souvenir hunters, I decided that caving was quite good fun. What could be more pleasant than a little demanding exercise, a spice of danger, plus a pleasing place in which to rest and appreciate nature's miracles before climbing back into the fresh air?

It was then that Tony said; 'Right! Let's move then,' and disappeared into an oversized rabbit hole, one characteristic of which struck me immediately. It led unmistakably and inexorably downwards. Nobody had told me – or if they had told me, I could not really have been listening – that our destination was a cavern 6,400 feet away from the entrance, and some 440 feet beneath the surface.

Already it was too late to turn back, and led by Tony Mintram I moved off into a passage in which a stoop rapidly changed to a crouch, a crouch into a crawl, and a crawl into what seemed at first sight an impossibility. Facing us in the light of our helmet lamps was a tunnel like a carelessly-made drainpipe, floored with small pools and loose rock and with the odd rock protruding from the sides to make it more interesting.

Tony Atkinson explained the technique to be used, while Tony Mintram demonstrated it. Lying flat on his stomach, with his arms fully extended in front of him, he used his fingers and toes to propel himself along the few yards of tunnel. Carefully I hitched my battery pack to the middle of my back and stretched out on the wet surface, looking forward to where my guide waited with the patience genuine experts almost always show for novices.

It was at this stage that I became painfully aware that, when it comes to caving, the extra five stone I was carrying over Tony's

44

A mile below the surface in a Mendip cave.

compact 9 stone 8 pounds was a considerable disadvantage.

Where the twenty-four-year-old bricklayer – known in caving circles as 'the Barnett Racing Snake' – had slithered with ease, I jammed myself firmly in a wedge of rock. I do not suppose I was stuck for longer than a couple of seconds, or even if my companions realised that I was stuck at all. It seemed longer at the time, though, long enough at least to savour the realisation that I was surrounded by several thousand tons of rock and likely to be there for a while unless I did something about it.

It is not exactly a relaxing situation, but the only thing you can do is to relax; allow rigid limbs and tense muscles to loosen up, and then crawl back an inch or so and try again. A couple of panicky moments – imagination is a useful tool for a thriller writer, but in some circumstances it can be a handicap – and I was through, and so filled with euphoria that I hardly noticed the near-sheer drop ahead – until I found myself doing the last couple of feet by the unrecommended free fall method, to the detriment of my battery pack. Then came quite a pleasant section, almost a stroll really, except for the broken and uneven surface and the occasional stretches not really meant for six-footers.

A rather steep climb down a near-vertical face with plenty of footholds saw the experts descending as if it had been a balustraded marble staircase with non-slip treads. To me it seemed a little more difficult, but eventually I was down in the rock-strewn passage leading to the main cavern.

Even in the sparse light from our lamps this was really something – a huge chamber with a wealth of stalactite formations and the constant sound of dripping water that is the background noise to all caving. Nothing disintegrates in caves, so nothing must be left. The only sign of human beings before us was a trace of carbide – and that in spite of the fact that the cave is a popular one.

At one stage we made the experiment of turning off our lights. It was an incredible Stygian black, literally like nothing on earth – and, as Tony Atkinson pointed out, an object lesson in why cavers should always check their batteries, and never go down alone.

Sitting there chatting, with only the occasional twinge of worry about small children who might be jumping up and down above our heads, I had almost forgotten the return journey.

'Always easier going up,' said Tony cheerfully; but he was not walking on legs made of plasticine.

Even with explicit directions and a lot of assistance in finding footholds, the climbs were hard going; at one stage I was glad of a hefty shove from below, and a genuine, fist-sized hand-hold that enabled me to slither over the crest. At that stage, anyone selling magic 'Get-you-to-the-surface Pills' at a hundred pounds a shot would have found a buyer; but, surprisingly, the narrow tunnel was less worrying now I knew I could get through, and after a few stiff scrambles we were in the small chamber. There I relaxed completely, which was a mistake because I had forgotten that I still had to move my near-fifteen stone some distance to the surface; apart from which my seven-pound battery pack was now weighing ten times its previous weight.

Somehow though, I struggled out and back to the roadway, even managing to clamber over the twenty-five-barred gate, and by the time we had got back to Tony's Red Lion a sense of achievement had overtaken tiredness, and that first pint of bitter was nectar.

While I drank I talked with Tony and some of his caving customers, who regularly brush up their skills by crawling through wire coathangers. I discovered that our cave was called GB, not because of any connection with Grievous Bodily Harm, which I had been quite willing to believe, but after Goddard and Barker, who dug it open in 1939.

I also discovered, from a book called *Mendip Underground*, that 'Mud Passage' is 'followed immediately by an awkward drop where a 30 foot line is a wise precaution'. On the other hand, my horrific slippery wall was 'an interesting fifteen-foot climb'.

Novice cave or not, I was pleased that I had gone down with two of the best cavers and teachers in the business; it is impossible to overemphasise the fact that nobody should attempt to go caving without at least one, or preferably two, experienced companions.

That being said, there are several excellent clubs on Mendip, including the Mendip Nature Research Station to which the two Tonys belong, and more than sixty named systems to explore, with names like the Coral Cave and Singing River Mine. Basic requirements, apart from good health and, I would say, a wiry frame, are a pair of stout boots, some old clothes and a boiler suit, a light and a helmet; clubs will normally lend the last three items for a trial run.

Later, enthusiasts can buy a rope and ingenious single-rope technique gear, metal clamps which slide easily up ropes but will

'Just like a big bird ...'

not slide down when pressure is put on them.

By this time, all nervousness forgotten, I was already preparing to cast myself in some heroic masculine mould, so it was hard on my male chauvinism to learn that Tony Mintram's wife and Tony Atkinson's ten-year-old daughter Nicola are both enthusiastic cavers, who regard GB as kid's stuff. Jason Atkinson, aged eleven, is also deeply involved.

'Are the children going to take it up seriously?' I asked Tony's wife, Irene. 'Not if I can help it,' she replied. 'I think they're all mad.'

Coincidentally, it was only about a mile away from the cave that I had the opposite, though equally off-beat, experience of flying in or on a microlight aircraft. Upstairs as opposed to Downstairs and, as I said in the Introduction, a splendid if somewhat unusual way of taking a good look at the Somerset countryside.

What I didn't mention was that I am usually one of those white-knuckle flyers who is convinced that if the Good Lord intended us to fly he would have made us a great deal braver than we are. That's why, on the day I tried out the microlight, I was astounded to find myself zooming around, hundreds of feet above the Cheddar Gorge with nothing but a canvas sling between me and the hard ground below – and enjoying every minute of it.

Hitherto the only aircraft in which I have felt really comfortable has been Concorde – perhaps because of its colossal power, perhaps because of the thought that people are liable to take extra care with a multi-million pound investment, but more likely because of the lavish hospitality to which I had been subjected both on the ground and in the air.

At Warren Farm, on top of the Mendips, there was not a drop of champagne in sight, and it was obvious that the caviar and vodka were going to be in short supply after takeoff; I did get half a cup of coffee and a biscuit while I looked over the aircraft, though.

To be honest, microlight aircraft do not look particularly robust to the uninformed eye. In fact, with their tubular frame, pram wheels, hang-glider wings and tiny engine they have something of a Heath Robinson air. The propeller looks like something from a child's toy, while the 'canard', the moveable surface at the front, seems almost an afterthought.

I had to remind myself that birds do quite well in the air, in spite of what seems to be a fragile construction. Anyway, it was too late to turn back, so togged up in my borrowed flying helmet, I struggled into the sling seat of the twin-seater microlight, buckled myself in and sat back while the test pilot and director of training, Paul Baker, explained the controls.

This did not take long, for apart from the throttle there is only a joystick, which you push forward to go down, pull back to go up, and right or left to go right or left. When left to its own devices, Paul explained, the aircraft adopts a comfortable nose-up position and cruises away on an even keel. To tell the truth, at this stage it all sounded a little hair-raising, and there did not seem any way the machine would lift a combined weight of twenty-five stone or so off the deck, less still keep it up and bring it back safely.

Then the engine was started on a string pull, somewhere behind

49

**'Microlight aircraft do not look particularly
robust ...'**

my neck a propeller not a lot bigger than the ones we used to use on
models began to whizz round, and we moved forward across a
stretch of damp, flat but by no means bowling-green grass. After
fifty yards or so the contraption took off and suddenly became
something quite wondrous, a perfectly-designed machine that was
now in its element. Icarus eat your heart out! Spitfire pilots move
over! This is real flying, moving with the air rather than fighting it,
yet in control by virtue of the tiny engine and that ingenious little
'canard'.

Over Cheddar, Paul pointed out a couple of birds that had flown
up to inspect us, like suspicious fighters.

Just a big bird; that is exactly how it feels, right down to the
swooping landing, which straightens out as the plane kisses the turf
and comes to rest in a couple of cricket pitch lengths. No sighs of
relief for me after touchdown, on this flight; given half the chance, I
would have gone up again, and again.

Junkers and Jumbos

Looking at Somerset from the seat of a microlight aircraft reminded me that the county's major airport was the scene of the zaniest inaugural flight of all time when a slight miscalculation on the part of the navigator precipitated a chain of events reminiscent of a Will Hay comedy.

The fact is that one of the first overseas flights to land at Bristol Airport was a Junkers 88 bomber of the German Luftwaffe, which dropped in by mistake in the early morning of 24 July 1941, after a bombing raid on Birkenhead. The pilot, Unteroffizier Wolfgang Hosie, had confused the Bristol Channel with the English one and thought he was landing at his home airfield near Brest.

As his machine came to a halt he noticed that there was a mechanical digger at work on the aerodrome, which was being prepared for RAF use, and addressed the driver of it in broken French. He was not much wiser when the driver ponderously answered him in the broadest Somerset, which he must have taken for an odd form of Gallic patois, and he was so involved with the resultant communications problem that he did not notice that the digger's mate had rushed off to fetch the military guard.

The Lulsgate site had been an RAF landing ground under the control of Weston-super-Mare, and its conversion for more important use began in May 1940. Runways were extended, and by March 1941, Messrs Northcote had begun to construct pillboxes and machinegun posts to defend the airfield from less confused visitors than the pilot of the Junkers 88.

The flight lieutenant who was adjutant at the time recorded the unexpected arrival of the Junkers and the primitive living conditions at Lulsgate for both officers and men – as well as enthusing on the loveliness of the Somerset countryside as seen from the air. Something of a poet, he was not averse to including a

51

stanza or two in his official report. He wrote as a tailpiece: 'The aerodrome is just one piece of England, one focus of all the tapestry of history out of the dim-most corridors of time.'

The particular corridor which led to Lulsgate becoming an important regional airport opened with the foundation of the Bristol Airplane Company in 1910 – a pioneering venture which was given tremendous impetus by the First World War, and which ensured that Bristol would take its place in the forefront of the new industry.

In 1927 a group of city businessmen raised £6,000 by public subscription to start the first flying club at Filton aerodrome, which was owned by the Airplane Company, and two years later the same group decided that Bristol ought to have its own airport. This led to an airport committee being formed, and farmland at Whitchurch was bought and developed.

Whitchurch was officially opened in 1930, at which time it was only the third civil airport in the country. It had everything,

Left: **Les Wilson, General Manager of Bristol airport.** *Below:* **Aircraft ancient and modern.**

including a terminal area, a hotel, a nine-hole golf course and, most important, room for expansion and extension of the landing areas.

In the first year 535 aircraft movements were recorded, with 929 passengers carried, and in 1932 came the first commercial foreign flights – eleven of them carrying eleven passengers, which gives some idea of the size of the aircraft involved. In 1936 came the first air freight – 500 kilos of it – and by 1939 there were 4,000 aircraft movements, 5,000 passengers and 3,000 kilos of freight.

At the beginning of the Second World War, though, Whitchurch was taken over by the Air Ministry, and became the only civil airport to remain open in the whole of the United Kingdom. From it, Imperial Airways, KLM and other lines that had moved from Croydon flew overseas services, including flights to Lisbon and the US via the Azores.

Throughout the war discussions were held on the peacetime future of the airport, but in the event it had no future at all, since aircraft designed to carry more than a handful of passengers were unable to land on grass, and the only hard runway at Whitchurch was incapable of extension.

In fact, although Whitchurch remained requisitioned, scheduled services were run from there until 1956, the year in which Bristol Corporation turned to Lulsgate, which had been disused for ten years. It was bought for £55,000, opened in 1957, and in its first year there were 15,000 aircraft movements, 33,000 passengers and 608,000 kilos of freight carried.

Extensions to the runway came in 1963 and 1969, when it was lengthened to 6,600 feet to take Boeings, Tridents, Comets and DC9s. At the same time the terminal was extended to cope with a sharp rise in passenger traffic, much of it holiday trade.

It was all a far cry from the Whitchurch opening in 1930, when the airport handbook advertised the Breda, a two-seater high-wing monoplane fitted with a de Havilland Gypsy engine, which could take off and land in a hundred yards, cruise at 95 miles-per-hour and cost £850 complete. This was about twice the cost of a Humber car.

In the same handbook Bristol City Lines were still advertising sailings from Bristol Old Docks to Philadelphia, Norfolk, Virginia and New York, though in his foreword the city's Lord Mayor, Councillor Walter Bryant, assured his fellow citizens that

'Merchant adventurers in their Airships will sail from Bristol in the clouds, enhancing the wealth and commerce of this fine city.'

Four decades later, though, not everyone was as optimistic or enthusiastic as Councillor Bryant, and typical headlines in the local press read: 'Lines Will Quit Airport – Unless Developments Carried Out', 'Airport Crisis', 'Airport Spreading Wings Too Far' and 'Neighbours and Planners Object'.

The neighbours' objections were largely on the grounds of low-flying and noise, and having ducked under the table to avoid planes while having dinner with friends at Felton Common, I can appreciate the problem.

In spite of protests, the runway was extended, even if it did prove inadequate for one pilot a few years ago, who took off for Karachi in a mystery Boeing 707 with false Zaire registration, leaving souvenirs of his aircraft on trees and perimeter lights. The pilot – a Mr Khan Junior, whose father owned the plane – was subsequently discovered to have wrongly loaded his 70,000 lb of fuel, and to be in possession of a revoked US commercial pilot's licence.

More suitably qualified pilots have had considerably less trouble in using the improved airfield on which more than a million pounds has been spent in recent years, and general manager Les Wilson anticipates 400,000 passengers this year.

Wolfgang, not to mention any other German tourists he might care to bring along, would be more than welcome, for the wartime airfield has been turned into a thriving concern making an annual profit of more than half a million pounds and employing some 400 people. Many of them work in franchise operations like the bar, restaurant and duty-free shop, which Wolfgang might find pleasantly friendly after the impersonal bustle of some of the major German airports. And if he is in business – manufacturing navigational equipment perhaps – he would doubtless be interested to learn that Bristol plans further improvements including a freight cabin to replace the present rash of portacabins.

Unlike most big international airports, Bristol still has something of the feel of a flying field about it. There are no umbilical tunnels joining the terminal to planes, and you are actually aware that you are climbing aboard an aircraft. This has the effect of making you feel more like a human who has elected to fly, rather than an object to be packaged and dispatched to its destination as impersonally as possible.

55

Relatively small though it is, Bristol can usually offer plenty to catch the eye from its balcony restaurant and bar. As well as watching the jets take off, waiting passengers can follow the progress of small monoplanes at the flying school, various air taxis and helicopters – and perhaps, as on several days this summer, something really exotic like the Goodyear airship, or Second World War veterans.

They could also, if they are lucky, see some unusual cargoes being unloaded. There is a tale, for instance, of an anxious group waiting to see a priceless Irish racehorse off the plane on his way to the Cheltenham Gold Cup meeting. When the doors opened, down came not a snorting thoroughbred but a demure donkey, who turned out to be the champion's constant companion, without whom he firmly declined to travel.

That's the sort of yarn you could expect from an airport which began with such inspired comedy and it leads one to hope that one day they could make full use of their very own Luftwaffe Pilot, 'Wrong Way Wolfgang'.

In fact that time may not be far off as the next stage in the Lulsgate expansion programme could entail flights to and from West Germany. 24 July would make an ideal day for the inaugural flight and the Germans would almost certainly be prepared to dig up a Junkers 88 from one of their aircraft museums and to fly it over Lulsgate, together with Wolfgang, if he's still going strong. He could unveil a bust of himself in the new terminal – facing the wall, of course – and no doubt the airport authorities would take advantage of the occasion to announce that in future the 24th of July will be known as Wolfgang Hosie Day.

Always provided that Wolfgang doesn't somehow contrive to land on the Costa Brava by mistake.

Bristol Airport '... can usually offer plenty to catch the eye from its balcony restaurant and bar.'

Singing Siblings

When Roger Bevan and his wife Cecilia took their children away from school to teach them at home they solved the question of music lessons by forming a choir.

It was an off-beat solution which was to have far reaching repercussions since in order to give their family choir a sense of purpose they decided to enter it for competitions in the Mid Somerset Festival at Bath. That was in 1956 and although the Bevan children did well Roger and Cecilia could hardly have dreamed that the Bevan Family Choir was soon to make its mark well beyond its own front parlour.

In fact the choir went from strength to strength and in the summer of 1978 made its London debut at St John's, Smith Square, following it up with a highly successful tour and an equally successful record – 'Music In The Family'. The title was apt because the eight to ten singers taking part were all brothers and sisters from the Bevan's fourteen strong family who had turned professional in 1970.

Their headquarters, and the family home, was – and still is – a rambling fifteenth-century farmhouse in the village of Croscombe near Wells, with two acres of land for vegetables, pigs, goats and chickens. It's an hospitable sort of house, too, where visitors can expect not only dinner but perhaps, if the children are visiting, an impromptu recital of madrigals.

When the children were growing up it was a house where most of the living was done in the huge farmhouse kitchen, where mother became mercifully deaf to the individual sounds of music practice and where the family's off-beat lifestyle was symbolised by the fact that, in self-defence, Roger Bevan had a pay telephone installed. It was the sort of move which, with enough children for a football

Just a few of the Bevan Family Choir gathered together once again at home for Christmas 1985.

team and three reserves, made a lot of sense, as did the rule that any of the children who quarrelled had to go outside.

When I visited the house I asked Roger about the choir's background. 'My father,' he told me, 'was a clergyman – the Archdeacon of Ludlow – and we were a musical family. I was a chorister in his church and took music at Shrewsbury. Later, when I was reading classics and theology at Oxford, our college organist joined up and I took his place.' Then, while serving with the Gunners in India, Roger kept up his musical interests by studying plainsong with the Jesuits – he had by that time become a Catholic – and by unlikely forays into the 'It ain't 'alf 'ot Mum' world of troop entertainment.

After the war he and his wife ran their own school until 1953 when he became director of music at Downside School near Bath. By then they had six children who were singing in three parts 'quite happily' and three years later they took up competitive singing. 'They came in second, without fail, each year,' he recalled.

In 1970 the choir – with several new additions from the family – turned professional, which meant that if they sang for a wedding they charged from £75 plus expenses, but very soon bigger money was in sight. For its European tour the choir that began by singing round the kitchen table was taking £200 a concert and being told by experts that they should have asked for twice that fee. Even so, money was still a problem because, like many professional artists, the older children were finding it impossible to abandon well-paid jobs and professions in order to devote themselves full time to the choir. In their case, too, the difficulty was compounded by the number of people involved, which made £200 for a concert seem rather poor pay.

The trouble was that some of the older members of the family were already living and working away from home. By 1978, for instance, David, the 27 year old tenor, was commuting between Britain and Minnesota where he was master of the Schubert Choir of St Paul, while the 26 year old soprano Rachel was a professional singer and a member of the London Oratory Choir, the Clerkes of Oxenford and the William Byrd Choir. Some of the other children were now living or working in London, while even those who lived locally, like Rupert the 23 year old baritone, had to fit in choir activities with their other posts – in Rupert's case as a horticulturist and as Choir Master of St Mary's Church in Bath.

For the younger members of the family there were also the demands of homework and exams but, in spite of all the difficulties, the critics continued to enthuse about the family choir's 'sensitivity', 'remarkable range', 'sense of style' and 'the intimacy and unity generated in a family group working together over the years'.

Other critics spoke of 'an almost telepathic sensitiveness', there was talk of sponsorship and a feeling that the Bevan Family Choir was going places. As Roger Bevan put it at the time, 'If we become really big we hope most of them would wish to be involved. Meanwhile they all have their own lives, their own jobs and exams. They can't afford to give up money making enterprises.'

Cecilia 'Mollie' Bevan never sang in the choir despite – or perhaps even because of – having a musical background. Her father was an opera singer, but she claims she was more influenced by her mother who was left a young widow and considered music to be an 'unsafe and insecure' profession. Musical or not, Mollie is the sort of person who takes everything in her stride; she had her fourteenth child Benjamin after celebrating her silver wedding anniversary, in spite of her son Jeremy's assurance that his prep school science master had told him it was 'quite impossible'.

Mollie's contribution to the family's musical life was limited to an occasional hymn on the piano but as she was usually out of practice any mistake was the signal for three or four pairs of hands to be thrust across hers to 'show her how to do it'.

Since I last met the family Mollie has written a charming autobiography called *Against All Advice* published by Parsonage Press, in which she tells the whole story of her off-beat life, starting with her nomadic childhood which in contrast to her cousin Roger's life at Quatford Castle was a mixture of haphazard schooling and hard work, training first to go into service and then to be a nurse, both of which stood her in good stead when she married Roger and started their production of the Bevan Family Choir.

'From the earliest days,' she recalls, 'the piano has been played all day long. As soon as one person got up from the stool another took his place. David's early attempts at "God Save The Queen" have been repeated by all his younger brothers and sisters. I soon ceased to hear the piano. Other people asked me if it didn't drive me mad but I think I only noticed if the house was empty and no one was playing.

'When Kathleen Long came to give a recital at Downside she stayed with us and spent much of her time playing to the children and when she left Tony, who was only three, started to play her pieces by ear, standing on the pedals with his chin just above the keyboard; he couldn't even see his hands.'

Although the piano was played all day long only one of the Bevan children pursued his piano studies to anything like professional standard although the family does include two professional organists and performers on the violin, cello, flute, oboe and bassoon.

'Their strongest point,' says Mollie, 'has always been singing, and especially choral singing.'

Summer in Somerset.

For years the Bevan Family Choir gave countless concerts, travelling to Germany, Holland and Denmark and appearing on television, but jobs and marriages – especially the latter – were taking their toll.

Nowadays it is rare for the whole choir to be together except for Holy Week services at Downside or for Midnight Mass, although recently they have made several TV appearances. Says Mollie, 'The married ones don't often sing at concerts but when for some reason they are all together at home I love to see them sitting round the kitchen table, joined perhaps by some visitor who can read music and singing just for the love of it.'

With twelve grandchildren at present there could be a new generation of the Bevan Family Choir but, for the moment, the kitchen table ensemble seems to be returning to its origins.

Combat Game

Those who know about such things claim that there is not much to beat a Westcountry infantryman – which is a reassuring thought when you are holding a defensive position against an advancing enemy.

Even so, as I lay behind the low ridge that was our only real cover, straining to hear the crack of a twig from the woods in front of us, I could not help reflecting that we were all green troops, as yet untried in battle.

As it happened, I need not have worried; when the shooting began, men like Tony Leonard, who in civilian life is a Bristol hairdresser, and his twenty-year-old son Paul behaved like veterans, keeping up a rate of fire that would certainly have kept the enemy at bay if the only trained soldier among us had not let the side down. The fact is that after loosing off a shot which brought down one of the opposition, I made such a mess of reloading that they were able to overrun our position, shooting me up pretty badly in the process.

Fortunately I had been gunned down in one of the very few battles after which wounds heal miraculously, the dead come back to life and there is a money-back guarantee to fall back on if you have not enjoyed yourself.

In my case I enjoyed the second battle better than the first, as by that time I had managed to work out the method of taping cartridges into a bundle to overcome the disadvantage of a single-shot gun. I suppose the chaps who tried to turn me into a soldier many years ago would not have been all that happy; but as I recall, they were not over-enthusiastic about my martial skills even then.

Perhaps it was just as well that our battle was in the game of Combat Zone – a new sport which is sweeping the Westcountry, both as a leisure pursuit and a management training tool. This

Above: **The battle ground.** *Right:* **Valerie Deane gets into the army way of life.**

means that apart from wounded pride, the worst that can happen is usually a splattering with yellow dye.

The special guns used in the game fire a dye-filled pellet that breaks on impact – and incidentally gives the game its motto *Who Dyes Wins.* They also add a great deal of realism, since being hit by a real missile is more impressive than being shot at with blanks.

Before the game started I talked to Rupert Phillips, aged 34, who runs the Combat Zone enterprise, and on whose 1,200-acre estate at Burnworthy, Churchstanton, near Taunton, the battles are fought.

'I don't know if there were ever any real hostilities on the estate, but there might well have been if the Germans had invaded in World War Two,' he said. 'As my father discovered when he reached Berlin with his armoured regiment, the Nazis planned to use it as their regional HQ, because of its water supply.

'We have been playing Combat Zone commercially since September 1984, and although we have not poured immense amounts of capital into it, numbers are increasing and players are making repeat visits. Soon we shall be converting some of the out-buildings to provide showers and changing rooms.

'We are also arousing interest among some of the big firms. Nabisco have already sent teams, and we have had inquiries from several Bristol banks, firms of solicitors and large commercial companies. People like this are using Combat Zone to test the leadership qualities of their executives, and to see how they behave under stress.

'When you are playing the game, someone has to lead, and it is interesting to find out how we all react under the sudden pressure of a combat situation. Funnily enough, SAS types are not invariably successful. They tend to run rings round the others for the first few games, but then the civilians learn how to work as a team.'

Waiting for the troops to assemble in the courtyard of the big house took me back to my army days, although not many of our chaps arrived at the assembly point in Porsches, and in those days hardly any soldiers wore fashion boots. There was the same feeling of *déjà vu* about the short trip in the personnel carrier which took us to within a hundred yards of the battleground. There were even the same sort of jokes as the tension began to build up.

Then, as we drew our guns and ammunition under the watchful eye of Combat Zone's sales director, Steve Davis, most of the wisecracking stopped; the talk turned to tactics and terrain, and the old sweats who were presumed to know the ropes were suddenly the focus of interest. The old hands, for instance, buy extra ammunition and tape the plastic pellet tubes together, enabling a practised shot to revolve a bundle round the barrel of the gun at a much faster rate than if he had to fumble in the pockets of his fatigues for every shot.

As we set off for our base camp in the woods the whole exercise was beginning to feel quite authentic, and I was glad to discover that my young partner, Valerie Deane from Salisbury, was a trained nurse.

The object of the game is to capture the opposing team's flag

Right: **A real taste of army food during lunch break.**

66

from their base camp and return to your own without being shot — which, in heavily wooded country, is not quite as simple as it sounds. In principle, the advantage should always be with the defence – and fighting a largely defensive battle to sap the enemy's strength would seem a sound tactic. In practice, however, soldiers show a reluctance to die, even if they know they will be resuscitated in time for the next battle.

Four observers control the game, each eqipped with CB radio. They start each battle with a blast on their hand-held air horns, and one of their jobs is to make sure, as far as possible, that soldiers who are killed stay dead. Still, as they cannot be everywhere at once, a really hard-pressed attack in force has a lot to be said for it.

On the day I was there, after the first game, when the new troops had learned how to use their guns and – vitally – how to reload and fire quickly, the advantage began to swing towards the defence: already a rough approximation of the Redcoat technique of one man firing while another reloaded was taking shape. Tactics will soon have to change, though, since the Japanese have now developed two types of pellet-firing machine guns, two pump guns and five types of pistol, including a machine version.

The game is changing in other ways, too. Rupert Phillips plans to put up a building in which terrorists can hold a hostage, for instance, and night operations are also on the cards. Meanwhile, there is already a trophy for the sport, presented by an enthusiastic trailer park owner, Bob Honeyfield. In spite of my ineptitude, it was won on my day by the Bristol team, trained by Andy Georgiou, an amusement arcade operator.

Now there is a chance that Combat Zone will spread to Mangotsfield, and eventually the HQ at Churchstanton will host comfortable 'getaway' weekend country house parties, where you shoot people instead of pheasants.

For the time being, meals are still taken with army realism from mess tins. After lunch, however, instead of the three 'rinse, wash and sterilise' tubs favoured by the army for washing up in the field, I found Rupert's girl friend, Lizzie Floyd, tackling a huge pile of mess tins in the mansion's scullery. I suppose even when you are paying to endure the rigours of battle, realism has to stop somewhere along the line.

Right: **The author in the Combat Zone.**

Cider Has Been The Ruin Of Us All

We British have always had a flair for pageantry, and by all accounts, the last public hanging in North Somerset was attended with the sort of pomp and circumstance that would have made the Trooping of the Colour look like the marchpast of a pack of Cub Scouts.

In those days one could still be hanged for stealing a handkerchief, but courts would usually avoid the death penalty, often by undervaluing the items stolen.

In the case of the three poor devils who played the leading roles in the drama enacted at Kenn, near Nailsea, on 8 September 1830, no such mercy was shown. Although their crime was the burning of three 'mows' of wheat worth £50, the real reason for their public execution was to discourage others from following their example. It was for this reason, too, that the executions were carried out at the scene of the crime, and staged to impress the crowds with what the *Bristol Mirror* for 11 September called 'the awful sentence of the law'.

No expense was spared to ensure that the three, thirty-five-year-old William Wall, thirty-two-year-old John Rowley and nineteen-year-old Richard Clarke were properly 'turned off'.

The procession, which left Ilchester Jail for Kenn, some forty-two miles away, was led by the chief constable on horseback, followed by a hundred stave-carrying special constables on foot. Then came the high sheriff on horseback, three magistrates and a chaplain in an open carriage, and a party of mounted 'Javelin Men with Halberds'.

Right: **Three poor devils hanged in public to discourage others.**

Next came the prison caravan, drawn by four horses and carrying not only the three criminals but also, in what seems a rather heartless touch, the governor of the county gaol, the executioner and his assistants. And bringing up the rear came a further party of javelin men, who were tenants of the high sheriff, and a troop of fifty mounted policemen.

After what must have been a difficult night march, much of it in pitch darkness and on bad roads, the cavalcade arrived in the village at about half-past ten, and was greeted by the tolling of the funeral knell. The procession halted in front of a house where the magistrates were assembled – having ridden ahead for breakfast – and Rowley was taken before them 'walking with a tolerably firm step' to make a full confession of his guilt.

Perhaps hoping for a last-minute reprieve, Rowley put all the blame on Wall and the strong cider he supplied. In fact, 'scrumpy' had a great deal to do with the men's predicament, as they had burned down the ricks in revenge for a £20 fine imposed on Wall for selling cider without a licence. He had a cider shop 'where young men of idle habits and bad character usually resorted'.

Farmer Benjamin Poole of Kenn was thought to have informed on Wall, and the rick-burning was said to have been his revenge. Rowley also confessed to knowing that a quarter of lamb they had dressed for their dinner had been stolen, but though he would have been unfortunate today to have been sentenced to anything much more severe than a few months – and suspended at that – his confession availed him nothing.

With Rowley back in the van the cavalcade moved off to a seven-acre field opposite the one where the mows had been burned, in the middle of which was a gallows bearing the notice 'For Firing Stacks'. There was no chance that the 15,000 onlookers would not get the message. The day was a Wednesday, usually a working day, which would have heightened the holiday humour normal on such occasions; no doubt the ballad sellers, food and drink pedlars and pickpockets had been busy since early morning.

The culprits were released from their fetters and bundled onto the scaffold where the chaplain, the Rev Mr Valentine, requested them to kneel down, gave each a prayer book, and had them repeat the whole of the Litany and several 'appropriate' prayers.

Wall was the first to be pinioned, and as he struggled to his feet he turned towards the magistrates and said: 'I hope, gentlemen, you will please to forgive my poor wife and children. Lord have mercy upon me! Christ redeem my soul!' He then repeated the Lord's Prayer, in which he was joined by Clarke and Rowley, and as the executioner and his assistants adjusted the ropes around their necks the three men read aloud from the prayer books they were still holding.

Wall again exclaimed: 'Pity my poor family!' – a request which, taken in conjunction with his excessive humility and piety in the face of those who were about to have him choked to death, makes it likely that a bargain had been struck.

Wall's wife, May, had been sentenced to death with her husband, as had Rowley's brother John; but they were both reprieved, and the sentence commuted to transportation, and this could well have been why, when the caps were about to be pulled over their eyes and they were asked if they had anything to say to the crowd, Rowley said only: 'I hope they will take warning by us.'

Wall added: 'I should not have been here if I had not opened a cider shop. If I had hearkened to my wife I should not have come to this.' And the young man Clarke exclaimed: 'Cider has been my ruin, and the ruin of us all!'

Then, as the special constables and the troops of the Bath and Bedminster Yeomanry Cavalry held back the crowd, the two-and-a-half hour show reached its climax, with the cart being drawn from under the three men.

Except for the lad, 'their sufferings appeared to be of short duration', but the unfortunate Clarke was too light for the rope to do its work, and after he had been 'slightly convulsed' for a while, two of the hangmen finished him off by swinging on his legs.

When the bodies had swung for an hour they were cut down and taken away in coffins, following which a local rector climbed onto the scaffold and gave a powerful address.

All in all, it was a thoroughly satisfactory morning's work for the Establishment, concluded just in time for luncheon. They must have felt that the peasantry had been taught an adequate lesson, though shortly afterwards the Bristol Riots were to prove them wrong.

Then, too, *al fresco* hanging was used to show the rioters the error of their ways, and on 27 January 1832, four men were hanged at the Drop at Bristol New Gaol for rioting. Before that there had been at least forty-three hangings in Bristol in the space of ninety years, most for murder but others for robbery, forgery and 'unnatural crime'.

Many of the executions were public. On 31 March 1793, a certain Shenkin Protheroe was gibbetted on Durdham Down, while on the same day George Game was hanged on Bedminster Down, thus providing the populace with both variety and gentle exercise. A drummer boy was shot on Brandon Hill, and three women were hanged for infanticide.

John Harwood, who was executed for murder on 13 April 1821, had the dubious privilege of christening the Drop at Bristol New Gaol, the scene of Bristol's last public hanging in 1849.

Sarah Harriet Thomas was an eighteen-year-old servant girl whose mistress had made her life intolerable even by the standards of the times; so much so that when she was condemned to death for killing the woman with a stone, thousands of Bristolians signed a petition to the Home Secretary urging her reprieve. None was forthcoming, though, and on 20 April 1849, Sarah was led out on to the Drop above the gate of the New Gaol in Cumberland Road.

As it was raining at the time, a member of the official execution party was deputed to hold a large umbrella over the condemned girl to protect her before the trap fell and left her kicking her life away at the end of a rope.

Meanwhile, thousands watched from the opposite side of the river, from boats and from the windows of rooms, specially rented for the occasion as she went through the lengthy ritual of prayer, pinioning and rope adjustment.

Like the Kenn arsonists, Sarah was the centre of attraction for the first and last time of her brief life.

A Minor Miracle

The Morris Minor, designed by Alec Issigonis, was a war baby, conceived in response to a brief to produce a small family car capable of a long production run; in fact, more than one million six hundred thousand of them were made before the end of the line in 1971.

Even then, the ladybird-shaped Minor – 'choose any shade as long as it's grey, green or black' – refused to die, and now, thanks to the Bath businessman Charles Ware, Britain's best-loved car is enjoying a new lease of life.

The Morris Minor Centre, where Charles Ware buys and sells Minors, rebuilds customers' cars, advises them on buying and runs an international mail order parts service, has a turnover of around a million pounds a year; now he plans to bring out a completely new Minor of his own.

The first Minors, produced between 1948 and 1950 as both saloons and convertibles, had headlights in the front grille and a split windscreen; they were powered by the 918 cc side-valve engine.

Later, headlights went up into the wings, the Traveller came in and, in 1956, the Morris 1000 engine was introduced. Other changes were – forgive the expression – minor, apart from 350 snazzy-looking lilac cars with interior white trim – the 'Morris Millions', with which the company celebrated its millionth Minor.

From 1964 the late Minors had a 1098 engine, ignition key start and a good heater, but by the early 1970s the solidly-built car proved too expensive to make when compared with the fast and comparatively luxurious 'tin boxes'.

Meanwhile, as inflation made it difficult for those without car allowances or tax concessions to buy new quality cars, Morris

Above: **At work on the Morris Minor.**
Right: **Charles Ware and Nick Harding.**

Minor owners began to realise that, while the cheaper modern cars were not only expensive but unreliable, their own vehicles were the Johnnie Walkers of the motoring world, capable of going strong for ever.

Even so, most owners believed that spares were running out and that their cars would be obsolete in two or three years. In 1977, though, amid the first rumblings of the energy crisis, Mr Ware opened his centre – and a year later Glass's Guide, the bible of the motor trade, confirmed the Minor's status as an investment car.

The newly-dubbed 'classic', however, more than earns its keep as a workhorse with its good starting, fuel consumption averaging 40 mpg, low-cost maintenance and durability. It is also competitive on country lanes because of its handling, but while it will reach motorway legal top speeds, its cruising speed is a modest 55 to 65 mph.

Prices range from about £600 for a car in need of restoration, through £1,300 for a decent runner with a guarantee and potential, to £3,500 or more for the top range of reconditioned models. Extras, like the reclining seats and luxury interior one customer ordered recently, could add another £1,000 but something around the cost of a new Mini should provide a car that will combine day-to-day transport with a reasonable investment.

Charles Ware himself is an appropriate man to be resurrecting the phoenix, for after being written off as a millionaire, he now seems on his way to his second fortune.

In the converted mill at Limpley Stoke where a few of the world's present stock of around a million Minors were being refurbished and prepared for the road, he told me: 'After studying and lecturing at the Slade I lectured at Bath Academy of Art and bought a house in the Royal Cresent in 1964.

'I became interested in building and became an enormously successful property man and builder. I was a millionaire for a short while – but it all went in the crash, because I was involved in building, rather than dealing. In March, 1975, I went bankrupt, owing just under half a million to banks and the like but no small debts – which meant I felt I could stay in the town. I didn't have to run away.

'I was completely cleaned out, but someone lent me a couple of hundred pounds and I started in the motor trade. I used to go to the motor auction at Westbury and buy old Minis and things. After a year of specialising in small cars I found that in the banger market you couldn't do much to something you were buying and selling cheap, so you had to buy one that worked; I soon discovered that the Morris Minors were the ones that always started in the morning, always did their job and had been going for a long time.

'That got me interested in the whole history of the Minor – why it went on and on and why it was a completely classless car owned by people in manors and people in council houses.

'I started specialising in 1976, and found that spares were available, even if they were a bit difficult to get hold of.'

Charles Ware insists that he went into the motor trade on impulse: 'What I didn't like, though, was the whole ethos of the trade, where the punter, the customer, came at the end of the line.

78

'The reason our business has got some sort of a name is that we work in exactly the opposite way to many people in the motor trade. We try to set out for people what things cost and why. Explanation is the name of the game, so if you can show people what actually happens and that you work at a certain rate per hour, they can see that everything has a logical relationship.

'We don't set out to make people spend a certain amount. We tell them what they ought to do to the car, give them a range of priorities if they have their own, and, if they're buying, tell them in exact detail what they are buying; if you have a range of cars from £500 to £8,000, things have to be made very clear.

'Now the motor trade has got fully involved with Morris Minors, which in some ways is a bad thing, because they're doing their usual thing of tarting up cars and trying to get high prices for mutton dressed up as lamb.

'We get a lot of help from British Leyland. They ask us what parts they should make and they are now going to manufacture a number of things they had previously stopped producing.

'We are also investing in remaking parts, and we now have a complete range.'

Since I first met him, Charles Ware has realised his dream – a Series 111 Morris Minor re-engineered for the Eighties which, while it looks very little different from the standard car, has surprising road manners and performance. The new off-beat Minor is a genuine Q-car – a wolf in Grandma's clothing, like the tramp steamer Q-ships of World War 1 whose innocent appearance concealed all sorts of anti-U-boat weaponry. Mind you, the modifications haven't been designed to turn the Minor into some kind of souped-up machine for boy racers. It's still a car for the family motorist but one who enjoys the look of incredulity on the faces of other motorists as the Minor cruises past them.

Motoring writers who tried out the prototype raved over the modifications which come in four 'packages' covering suspension, brakes, drive train and interior and can be installed separately or all at the same time. They rated its handling and performance as 'way beyond the imagination of a standard Minor owner' and ahead of typical modern hatchbacks like the Fiesta or the Astra.

The car cruises easily at motorway speeds and the braking is described as impressive – even 'miraculous' – which, for a car that will not have lost any of its value at the end of ten years, as compared with a normal car's loss of 82 per cent in six years, makes it an interesting proposition.

Even more interesting, from my point of view, is the prospect of fitting a 1.3 litre engine or something even more powerful into the re-engineered Minor instead of the uprated 1098 cc unit.

My most off-beat car to date has been an ancient open Ford V8 which looked like a biscuit tin on wheels but which could out-perform almost anything on the road, provided you didn't require it to stop.

The Series 111 Morris Minor, on the other hand, is an off-beat car which is also safe and economical so I may well put my name down for a Series 111 GTI – a vehicle which is already on the drawing board. After all, a 100 mph plus Morris Minor convertible with handling and brakes to match would be a very amusing way of getting around.

Meanwhile, says Charles Ware, the Centre can offer 'a series of different engines depending on whether people want the ultimate in economy or the sort of performance we have obtained, for instance, by fitting a Sprite engine.'

Ex-army officer, ex-teacher, ex-property millionaire Ware rolls his own smokes but drives an elderly but potent Mercedes when he is not behind the wheel of a Minor. He is certainly in business to make money, and I would estimate his chances of becoming a millionaire for the second time – 'making money's easy once you know the secret' – as more than fair.

On the other hand, customers and their vehicles seem to mean at least as much to him as profits, and if anyone were to ask me: 'Would you buy a second-hand car from this man?' my answer would almost certainly be: 'Yes.' Perhaps that, after all, is the real secret of how to make an off-beat million – or two.

The Butler Did It

There is a £1 million barn down at Eastwood Manor Farm in East Harptree – and if you want to know who was responsible for building it, the answer has to be: 'The butler did it.'

In this case the butler was a rather unusual domestic by the name of William Taylor. As butler to Sir William Gourney of Gourney Court, he wooed and won the master's daughter, and with her the considerable family fortune. But then, instead of following the classic fictional pattern and squandering the lot, he began farming in earnest, and obviously with a feeling that he had to impress his neighbours; certainly when he decided to build a new barn for the home farm of his new estate money was no object.

All of this was good news for Robert Smith, one of the keenest minds in agriculture in the nineteenth century, who was looking for someone to commission the farm building that was to be his masterpiece. Smith had begun as a farmer in Rutland, but later worked for Francis Knight at Emmet's Grange on Exmoor. His task was to help Knight develop his model farms by enclosing, improving and planting, but mainly by designing improved buildings for sheep and cattle. Later he moved to Chew Magna to work as a surveyor, and it was there that he met Smith, whose need to impress and means to do so coincided with his own wish to build the nonpareil of farm buildings.

The barn, which covers one and a quarter acres of ground, cost £1,500 to build in 1860 – the equivalent of some £1 million in today's money. The ex-butler got his moneysworth, though, both in impressive looks and utility – so much so that 120 years later the exterior has more of the air of an abbey than a barn, while inside is the flourishing centrepiece of a thriving farm.

Purists are still arguing over whether the building, with its handsomely proportioned stone façade, is predominantly Victorian or Regency in design, but to the layman's eye it has a great deal of the railway station Gothic which delighted Brunel. In fact, I feel that had Brunel been commissioned to design a barn this might well have been his answer.

There is the same delight in pure size, the same insistence on the finest of materials and the same combination of the aesthetic and the practical that characterises the work of the great engineer. There is also the same implication that the architect was designing a monument intended to last.

One small piece of frivolity is the siting of two meticulously carved stone sheaves at each end of the building, but a decorative belfry had a practical purpose; the farm labourers of the late nineteenth century were usually too poor to afford watches, but were nevertheless required to be punctual.

Mr Alfred Gay, who now farms the 340 acres of Eastwood Manor, uses the barn to the full and remembers his grandmother

The Million Pound Barn.

Mr Alfred Gay.

talking about the building: 'When it was built, my mother's mother was a little girl going to school at Chewton Mendip. She lived at Greendown, and her father used to take her to school with a horse and gig. On the way back he'd pick up stonemasons from off Mendip who were coming down here to work.

'They'd originated with the Cornish who'd worked on the tin mines in Cornwall and had come to Mendip to build the chimneys of the lead mines. They said they were working for a penny a day.'

It seems that the old lady's girlhood memories were at fault because, even considering the low wages of the time, a penny a day would have been scandalous. What is likely is that she misheard when her father told her the masons were on a penny an hour, which would give them something close to the abysmal agricultural wage of the time.

What Taylor saved on wages must have been spent on material.

As we walked up the solid stone steps and into the cloister-like second floor, Mr Gay explained that all the woodwork was Baltic pine, with the flooring tongued and grooved with inch metal to prevent grains from falling through. 'The doors are oak – from the estate – with countersunk screws and Samuel Newman locks,' he continued. 'The same locks are fitted to the separate feed stores and each door, from 1 to 50, has its own lock, the key for which was kept on a numbered board in the office. The carter, the shepherd, the stockman and the game-keeper each had his own key, so there was no question of one man "winning" another man's stores.'

Sums worked out in pencil on the backs of the doors show that the men took the system seriously, and it is amusing to think that the ex-butler with experience of stores going adrift may well have been the one to devise the system.

The two bullock yards each had a fountain to provide drinking water and one still remains, though the feeding bins have gone; instead of 25 animals in each shed, 105 dehorned cattle wait briefly in the pens to be milked. Over their heads hangs a network of what appear to be dangling strings, and I naively wondered what quaint Victorian farming custom had spawned them. In fact they turned out to be a recent addition to the amenities. 'My son Geoffrey thought it up,' said Mr Gay. 'Some of the cows are reluctant to come through to the parlour, especially those down at the farm end, if they have a tongue full of grass and don't want any cake.

'He has fixed up these strings of electric fencing, and when he gives them a touch with the current they soon come in. It is harmless, of course, and it can make twenty minutes' difference in milking time, as well as saving an extra hand.'

Like the wires, most features of the building have a purpose, even though it is not always apparent, even to a farmer. For instance, the covered entrance is floored with flagstones; each one, I learned later, has its own Roman numeral to ensure perfect fitting – but a six-foot length opposite the main doorway remains unpaved.

'About fifty years ago, when I used to come here with my uncle I asked him why they didn't finish the job,' Mr Gay recalled. 'He told me that the horses used to push the wagonloads of hay back into here, but of course a horse couldn't push a wagon backwards on flagstones. It had to have something to dig its heels into, so they left that bit unfloored.'

In its early days the huge barn was virtually a self-contained farm, with a flax mill, a cider press and a threshing machine as well as stalls, hay lofts and stables. All the machinery was driven through a water wheel which powered the drive shaft running the full length of the building. Then came steam power, which was followed by an oil engine in 1896, and a diesel in 1927 – a series of moves which, in view of today's fuel prices, seem distinctly retrogressive.

In addition to what must be the world's most unusual barn, Eastwood Manor Farm has a blacksmith's shop with all the fitments and tools of a hundred years ago, and a three-ton weighbridge on which the villagers could check, on payment of a farthing, the coal they had bought at Farrington Gurney.

Pride of place, however, goes to an immense wooden trolley, made in around 1900, which could carry ten 17-gallon churns of milk. The milk was delivered to the station on it and sent off to Cardiff, where it fetched $2\frac{1}{2}$d a gallon. 'The story is that in that way the trolley made enough money to buy this farm,' said Mr Gay. If so, the trolley saved an historic monument because it was Alfred Gay, the grandson of the trolley-owner who bought it, who realised that this building was unique. He insisted that it should be restored, at a time when the Ministry of Agriculture was advising its demolition – and in the years since he has never regretted that decision.

In fact, he has since discovered that in building the immense barn the enterprising butler was a hundred years ahead of his time. 'I was sent a copy of *The Times* published in 1868,' he told me. 'It contained a report about the intended sale of Eastwood Court which detailed Smith's reasons for building the barn the way he did. His sole ambition, it seems, was to get all his cattle under cover in bad weather in order to stop the grass being trampled into mud and to allow it to grow better – as well as making it easier for the men to tend the stock. In those days most people left their cattle out all year round because there was rarely any housing for them. Smith's expensive barn enabled him to keep more cattle for less cost and he did it by using methods we started moving towards at the end of the Second World War. His methods worked well then and I'm still using his barn in the same way today.'

You can't help feeling that the far from ordinary butler who made the transition from 'Downstairs' to 'Upstairs' would have been proud of his off-beat monument.

Saturday's Child

'I'm sorry,' Mrs Peggy Nisbet told her American caller. 'I'm afraid we can't make Margaret Thatcher wiggle.'

She replaced the receiver with calculated firmness.

'Would you believe it?' she exclaimed. 'That was a call from Ohio. They've just got to hear about our Mrs Thatcher doll, and say we could sell fifty thousand in America if we could make her wiggle or fit her up with a series of outfits. When I said we couldn't do that, they suggested we might make her smile when she was squeezed.'

Of course dolls from the House of Nisbet, as Mrs Nisbet explained, do not wiggle. In fact they do not move at all, but merely gaze out at you, usually from glass-fronted cabinets, looking every inch the splendid collectors' items they are.

I said I hoped the Americans were suitably chastened, and was rewarded with a dazzling smile. 'It's a good job I was fairly polite,' she added. 'They didn't tell me until half way through that they were phoning from a Cleveland radio station, and I was on the air.'

We were sitting in the study of Mrs Nisbet's home in Weston-super-Mare, and the call was the first indication that this was no standard-issue white-haired granny. At seventy-one, she coped with those tricky transatlantic queries like a young tycoon.

Of course ordinary grannies do not build up their charming hobbies into industries with a turnover of half a million pounds a year, either – and earn themselves an MBE for services to export in the process. It takes brains and courage for that – and Peggy Nisbet has both.

Right: **Mrs Peggy Nisbet.**

She was born in Bristol, but moved to Weston with her widowed mother when she was only a few months old, and lived there until she was nineteen. 'I didn't play with dolls a great deal when I was a young girl, not even as much as my sister did,' she said. 'But I always dressed them, and I think that's probably an indication of what I like doing now. It's the costuming I enjoy.

'When I was nineteen I went to London to get a job with the old London Omnibus Company. Later it became London Transport, and I was made secretary to Lord Ashfield, the chairman.

'Then I married a chartered accountant. He died in 1959, but we had started this business before then, because the children were at school. We needed some extra income, and by that time I was very interested in doll-making.

'During the war I was a cashier at Barclays Bank in Weston, and later I went to Bristol Pottery. From there I used to visit Stafford, where I helped select designs for tableware.

'In Coronation Year I decided that I would like to do a figure of the Queen in china or bisque. In dressing it I had to guess what the coronation robes would be like, and I did so almost exactly. A reproduction of the State Crown was made by a local jeweller.

'I think the dolls cost about £10. We do similar figures now for around £50 or £60, but I can never find one of the originals. I keep on advertising, but I've never been able to find one, and my prototype was destroyed by fire. I took the doll to Harrod's, and they took the whole of the edition of five hundred. That was the first I ever did.

'Then I started thinking. At that time I used to go over to France with the children. We had friends there, and they used to give me little dolls from Normandy, Brittany and so on. We had nothing like them over here, so I wasn't able to give anything back. It was then that I decided to do something about it.

'The first range I did was of six hundred historical dolls. I added some in European national costumes, and started visiting buyers. The business grew, but I realised that we needed a doll of our own which would have to be specially designed.'

At the time Mrs Nisbet was working in her own home and teaching the craft of sewing dolls' clothes to her outworkers.

'I had an aunt Kate who was a most beautiful needlewoman, and the two of us used to sit down and do all the first samples. The business was very small indeed. Soon it became obvious that we were going to have to form a company, and a businessman friend of ours from Bristol said he would come in as long as we were serious about it.'

Mrs Nisbet soon proved her point, showing at international toy fairs in Europe and America. Now the House of Nisbet factory on the Oldmixon Trading Estate at Weston employs about forty people and around a hundred outworkers, while Mrs Nisbet works mainly from home.

'We have a collectors' market,' she explained. 'In America, for instance, the collectors' clubs are very sophisticated, and collecting has become an industry, with conventions attracting more than 1,500 delegates. I make a list of characters about a year in advance, and then talk it over with my daughter and son-in-law. He is now the chairman of the company, and my daughter works on the design side.

'I design the dolls here at home with the help of an assistant. We make up paper patterns, then a first machine set, and then a finished doll. When it goes down to the factory it ceases to be my problem; you might say I get the nice bit.'

It was not always so, though, as her daughter, Alison Nisbet Wilson, explained down at the factory. 'In 1970 the factory burned down completely, and I told her: "Well, Mum, you've had a good run – why don't you take it easy?" Instead she said: "I'm not going to let a fire beat me," and set to work to build it up bigger than before.'

When I met her, Mrs Nisbet was working on designs for a history of modern fashion, using the creations of famous designers like Worth, and dolls of the people for whom they designed the clothes.

Meanwhile, at the factory, the latest line was the Nisbet Victorian Birthday Doll series, inspired by the nursery rhyme 'Monday's Child Is Fair Of Face'. As one of the dolls, a uniformed maid holding a feather duster, looks distinctly like a younger version of the firm's founder, I was not too surprised to discover that Mrs Nisbet had been born on a Saturday.

As the rhyme says, 'Saturday's Child Works Hard For a Living'.

Quite so.

Genuinely Off-Beat Somerset

It was the sight of a flock of bright orange sheep that led Lizzie Cox to take up the somewhat outré occupation of field watching and to spend a whole year studying a single field.

To the uninitiated it sounded a curious obsession and I remember suggesting when I went to interview her for television in the field at Nettlecombe, near Taunton, that her behaviour was, to say the least, eccentric. That of course was before she told me the whole story of her love affair with the field and demonstrated the unique work of art which resulted from it.

It developed, she told me, from her spontaneous reaction to the combination of bright orange sheep, complementing the blue sky as they moved vertically and horizontally across a hot dry stubble field and the sudden change to stormy grey skies and green growth after the drought. She was so moved and excited by what she saw that she began to record what was happening in detail and for the whole of the following year made a diary of drawings and photographs of the field in all its many moods.

It was then that she conceived the off-beat notion of putting the living, changing field into a box, a project which was to challenge all of her artistic talents. She began by making the structure – an eight foot by eight foot open-fronted box with its walls, floor and ceiling covered in layers of printed fabric, the colours of which reflected natural changes in the landscape and farming activities like ploughing, seeding and harvesting.

Lizzie designed, dyed and printed all the fabrics in her Nettlecombe studio, a stone's throw from her chosen field, and gradually worked out the mechanics of what became an immensely sophisticated system by which the field could be made to change its aspect as the cycle of the year progressed. The work involved a tremendous amount of sewing, followed by a great deal of trial and

**Dancer Kirstie Simson '... who gave an
incredible performance as a combination
puppet and puppet master ...'**

error experimentation as she devised slip-knots, pockets and pulley
systems and fitted thousands of press stud fasteners and yards of
disguised Velcro. It also took a lot more time than Lizzie had
anticipated and it was May 1979 before the box was completed.

At the time Lizzie, who is a trained mime artist, intended
performing in the box herself since the changing fabrics followed
the changes in the field and didn't need to be choreographed. She
felt that Nature and the farmer were providing their own
choreography with the movements of the sheep, crows and seagulls;
the harrowing, ploughing and so on. They were all natural rhythms
which she was certain her mime experience would enable her to
follow.

In the end, however, she decided that her acting and dancing
skills didn't measure up to her professional abilities as an artist and
print maker and that if these were to be complemented to the best

advantage she would need the help of a professional dancer. She would also, she realised, need a special piece of music for the performance and composer Stuart Gordon – who, having lived in Nettlecombe, appreciated both the landscape and her project – agreed to write it for her. A couple of months later she met Kirstie Simson who was so taken with the box that she soon became completely involved in the performance and for the next five months artist, dancer and composer worked together on refining the movements, the fabrics and the music.

Then in March 1980, some four years after Lizzie's first glimpse of the orange sheep, 'Somerset' was performed for the first time.

'Inside the small fabric box,' wrote one critic, 'it is September 1976 and the end of a long, high, hot summer. In the sunlight the sheep glow orange, amidst the stubble of a harvested field. Soon the bright colour will be washed away in the outburst of rain that has been so long awaited, and for an hour the annual cycle of life in this Somerset field will be created in visual collage of dance and music.'

I have to confess that my attitude to most modern art is based on a compound of Philistinism, ignorance and deep suspicion. In fact I began my TV interview with Lizzie by poking gentle fun at her for being the sort of nut who would spend a whole year looking at a field. However, within minutes I had been completely won over by her professionalism and obvious sincerity, although I was still a little apprehensive in case the performance of 'Somerset', which I was scheduled to see later, proved to be 'arty' and incomprehensible.

As it turned out I need not have worried because the performance worked on any number of levels, fascinating young children as well as professional art critics. I thought it was delightful, with Kirstie giving an incredible performance as a combination puppet and puppet master, dancing and manipulating the fabric clad walls of the box which could have been either a small theatre or an oversized television set, but which became simply – a field.

Critics praised her dancing and Stuart's music as doing much to develop 'the abstract qualities of this beautiful work' but then they had not seen the original field, as I had. There were abstract patterns of course but in general the performance was a colourful narrative, with Lizzie herself, who had spent the whole hour helping with costume changes and props, entering the field for the

**'She felt that Nature and the farmer were
providing their own choreography ...'**

last scene to bring to an end the year she had observed so
closely.

It was an hour into which the changes of the seasons were
compressed so that the audience experienced a rapidly changing
series of moods and a myriad blues, greens, greys, reds, yellows and
browns – not to mention the orange of the sheep.

In fact I was quite prepared to believe Lizzie when she told me
later, after 'Somerset' had been successfully performed hundreds of
times, that when she and Kirstie were 'putting the box back', as

93

they called it, they still felt relief as they left the brown winter fabrics behind for the new greens of the spring growth.

In a way, I suppose, the story of the girl who spent a whole year studying a single field turned out be not quite as zany as it sounded, so the fact that the performance of 'Somerset' itself was visually pleasing was a compensation.

There was another – a remarkable piece of serendipity which arose as I was driving away from Lizzie's studio, past the gates of Nettlecombe Court a hundred yards or so down the road. By the gates stood an imposing official notice announcing that the manor was the headquarters of 'The Field Studies Council' – an august academic organisation with no connection whatsoever with Lizzie and her field – a coincidence that was pure off-beat Somerset.

Also Available

UNKNOWN BRISTOL
by Rosemary Clinch
Introduced by David Foot, this is Bossiney's first Bristol title. 'Rosemary Clinch relishes looking round the corners and under the pavement stones ...'
'... with its splendid introduction by David Foot, peeps into parts of Bristol that other books do not, and I can hardly do better than steal from David's introduction a quote from that great journalist, the late James Cameron, who declared to the editors of the many papers for which he worked, "If you want the facts, you can get 'em from Reuters. I'll look beyond the facts for you." In her own way this is exactly what Rosemary Clinch has done for Bristol ...'
Heidi Best, Somerset & Avon Life

UNKNOWN SOMERSET
by Rosemary Clinch and Michael Williams
A journey across Somerset, visiting off-the-beaten-track places of interest. Many specially commissioned photographs by Julia Davey add to the spirit of adventure.
'Magical Somerset ... from ley lines to fork-bending; a journey into the unknown ... a guide which makes an Ordnance Survey map "an investment in adventure".'
Western Daily Press

CURIOSITIES OF SOMERSET
by Lornie Leete-Hodge
A look at some of the unusual and sometimes strange aspects of Somerset.
'Words and pictures combine to capture that unique quality that is Somerset.'
Western Gazette

GHOSTS OF SOMERSET
by Peter Underwood
The President of the Ghost Club completes a hat-trick of hauntings for Bossiney.
'... many spirits that have sent shivers down the spines over the years ...'
Somerset County Gazette

EXMOOR IN THE OLD DAYS
by Rosemary Anne Lauder. 147 photographs.
The author perceptively shows that Exmoor is not only the most beautiful of our Westcountry moors but is also rich in history and character: a world of its own in fact.
'... contains scores of old photographs and picture postcards... will provide a passport for many trips down memory lane ...'
Bideford Gazette

SOMERSET IN THE OLD DAYS
by David Young. 145 old photographs.
David Young of TSW takes a journey in words and old pictures across Somerset.
'Scores of old photographs of good quality and high human interest... Excellent value... It is narrated by David Young, Television South West's architectural pundit, and his captions are usually eye-catching and informative.'
Drew Brodbeck,
Gloucestershire and Avon Life

STRANGE SOMERSET STORIES

Introduced by David Foot with chapters by Ray Waddon, Jack Hurley, Lornie Leete-Hodge, Hilary Wreford, David Foot, Rosemary Clinch and Michael Williams.

'Publisher Michael Williams has tried to capture an essence of the Westcountry bizarre ...'

Peter John,
Bath and West Evening Chronicle

LEGENDS OF SOMERSET

by Sally Jones. 65 photographs and drawings.

Sally Jones travels across rich legendary landscapes. Words, drawings and photographs all combine to evoke a spirit of adventure.

'... an entertaining look at county tales that have long inspired chill or chuckle.'

Somerset County Gazette

THE QUANTOCKS

by Jillian Powell with photographs by Julia Davey

'Seen from Taunton or The Mendips, the Quantocks look timeless ...'

Sensitive combination of words and pictures produce a delightful portrait of the area.

WESTCOUNTRY MYSTERIES

Introduced by Colin Wilson

A team of authors probe mysterious happenings in Somerset, Devon and Cornwall. Drawings and photographs all add to the mysterious content.

'... unresolved stories from past and present. Most beguiling is David Foot's essay on Thomas Shoel, the 18th century composer from Somerset. I would buy the book for that story alone ...'

Margaret Smith, Express and Echo

HEALING, HARMONY & HEALTH

by Barney Camfield

Healing in its various forms, the significance of handwriting and dreams, and psycho-expansion.

'If you are tuned in to the right wave length of new age thinking... you won't want to put it down until you get to the last page.'

David Rose,
Western Evening Herald

We shall be pleased to send you our catalogue giving full details of our growing list of titles for Devon, Cornwall and Somerset and forthcoming publications.

If you have difficulty in obtaining our titles, write direct to Bossiney Books, Land's End, St Teath, Bodmin, Cornwall.